The Boy and the Bomber

The Boy and the Bomber

A downed Lancaster, her crew and those who came to their aid.

Francois Ydier

Published in France as *L'Enfant et L'Avion*

Bomber Command Books
from
Mention the War

First published in the United Kingdom 2016 by Mention the War Ltd., Leeds, LS28 5HA, England.

Cover design: Topics - The Creative Partnership www.topicsdesign.co.uk
Cover image: Francois Ydier.

A CIP catalogue reference for this book is available from the British Library.

ISBN-13: 978-0993336058

ISBN-10: 0993336051

Other Bomber Command books from Mention the War

Striking Through Clouds – The War Diary of 514 Squadron RAF
(Simon Hepworth and Andrew Porrelli)

Nothing Can Stop Us – The Definitive History of 514 Squadron RAF
(Simon Hepworth, Andrew Porrelli and Harry Dison)

A Short War – The History of 623 Squadron RAF
(Steve Smith)

RAF Bomber Command Profiles:
103 Squadron
617 Squadron
(Chris Ward)

A Special Duty – A Crew's Secret War with 148 (SD) Squadron
(Jennifer Elkin)

Lancasters at Waterbeach – Some of the Story of 514 Squadron
(Harry Dison)

Skid Row to Buckingham Palace
(Ed Greenburgh)

The above books are available through Amazon in print, Kindle and, eventually, audio book format. For further details or to purchase a signed and dedicated copy, please contact *bombercommandbooks@gmail.com* or visit www.bombercommandbooks.com

About the Author

François Ydier was a small boy when the war came to his French village of La Celle-Les-Bordes. The crash of Lancaster MkII DS822 of 514 Squadron RAF had a significant and long-lasting effect on the community. After VE Day, his father took him to see what remained of the wreckage, asking François to stand alongside the tail to give a sense of scale as he took a photo (see cover).

Aviation entered François' blood and in the Sixties he gained a pilot's licence. He is a graduate of Supaero University. He worked in the French aerospace industry (including the Concorde programme) until the early seventies, flying on many planes and making a number of parachute jumps. Francois then developed his career in the marine and oil industries.

In his spare time and then retirement, François researched the stories of the crew of the Lancaster and those who helped them, including members of the Resistance and those who helped run the famed 'Comet Line', dedicated to helping downed airmen evade capture and return to England. Whenever possible, he attends the annual reunion of 514 Squadron members and families.

François still lives in the Paris area and Basque country with his wife Françoise.

Acknowledgments

I would like to present here my greatest thanks to all those who offered spontaneously their help, actively participated in the research for building a true story and put together the pieces of the puzzle with a special mention to the outstanding help brought by Anne Francoise DUTHEILLET de LAMOTHE, Carl LEWIS and Stan KERSHAW in proof reading and cautiously correcting the English text.

I apologise in advance for those I could have had forgotten, the help received having been so important! In doing so, we went much further than we imagined in our greatest dreams. On many occasions, facts were revealed as if we had been guided...

Francine AUGER, André BILLARD, Christiane and Jacques BLUANLUET, Thierry BOCHE, Roger BOSCHET, Neil BRYAN, Johnny BOULE, Thierry BOCHE, Elvire de BRISSAC, Neil BRYAN, Carl LEWIS, Bob CARMODY, Philippe CHALLE, Daisy CLARKE, Jean Michel COUDRAIS, Lucienne and Jean DASSIÉ, Gillian DEAN, Monique DACHEUX (DEVILLIERS), Marc and Yvonne DARBONNE, Lucienne DASSIE, Henri DEVILLIERS, Géraldine CERF de DUDZEELE, Christian DULAUROY, Anne Françoise DUTHEILLET de LAMOTHE, Theresa EDGAR, Daniel FLAHAUT, Roger GUERNON, Ed GREENBURGH, Simon HEPWORTH, Jean HUON, Maurice JAMES, Roger JOUSSAUME, Henri KERGREIS, Stan et Beryl KERSHAW, Josephine KOLLMANNSBERGER, Christie LAMASON, Michel LEBLANC, Annick LEHMAN, Josselyne LEJEUNE-PICHON, Christiane LETEISSIER, Clive LEWIS, Sargeant Piper LOPEZ, Becky MAC NAUGHTON, Elisabeth and « Pampi » MENDIBURU, Claudine and Phillippe MERLINO, Phillip MOUNTSTEPHEN, Alain POPULAIRE, Ngaire NYSTRUP, Simone OLIVIER, , Martine and Paul POISSON , Antoine POLIET, Andrew PORRELLI, Serge QUERARD, Solange and André RAFFRAY, Noreen RIOLS, Ydoine RIVIERE, Anne-Marie SANDERSON, Violet REITH, Jean et Sinclair RONALD, Joelle and Nicolas RUELLE, Perrine SAVERI, Marie-Pierre SAVILLE, Marie Laure de ST EXUPERY, Bill SHEPPARD,

Suzanne SIFFROI (DAIFELI), Serge SIREAU, John TANNEY, Lisa Ydoine and Alex TODD, Paul STOUFFER, Bernard TONDEUR, Ferdinand YDIER, Pierre YDIER, Kenneth WRIGHT,

On Saturday, March 28th 2015, a working session was organised in Moulin des Clayes, Joelle and Nicolas RUELLE's home, with Geraldine CERF de DUDZEELE, Josselyne LEJEUNE PICHON, Roger GUERNON, Antoine POLIET and myself. The purpose of the meeting was to make the last corrections to the text before printing the book...

ooooooooooooooooooooooooooooooooooooo

Contents

Preface

This book is dedicated to all United Kingdom, Allied and Commonwealth airmen for the outstanding role they played during WWII. They came spontaneously in great numbers to fight the Nazis. We owe to all these brave men our freedom to day and we have to keep alive their memory. Nothing had prepared them to face such difficult situations and we must remember what they accomplished.

I am not trying to make an apology for war; there is no such thing as a good war. Thousands of stories like this one occurred in the Forties.

These heroes - they were all heroes - demonstrated an exceptional courage and determination which deserves our admiration. We should not forget their families either. They, without any doubt, not only forged the courage and the character of these men, but also shared their pains. We should not forget their feelings when one of them was reported missing, without the family knowing what happened. Ydoine Riviere understood perfectly well their situation, her behavior is a perfect example of what could be done to help. May all their families be thanked and honoured in their turn.

Over fifty five thousand RAF airmen died in Bomber Command between 1939 and 1945[1]. We have to realise that and not forget their sacrifice. By comparison with media reporting of today's war casualties, I think sometimes they are doing too much. The world has definitely changed, I don't think such wars of extermination would be possible today, which is major progress in a way.

Airmen of Bomber Command completed a tour of operations after thirty combat missions (thirty six after D-Day), and would often be posted to less demanding duties, or back to their home countries. Some volunteered for a second and sometimes third tour. They were not flying every day, but sometimes twice a day, in particular after D-Day. So many of them were reported missing that, at the end, airmen did not even try to build friendship with others within their squadron.

---

[1] Chorley: RAF Bomber Command Losses 1939-45. RAF 38,462; RCAF 9,919; RAAF 4,050; RNZAF 1,679; Polish Air Force 929; Other Allied air forces 473; South African Air Force 34; others 27.

The Boy and the Bomber

Their routine was a constant situation of Fear and Hell. Flying in the dark seven hours at 20,000 ft. above clouds to escape flak shells with an outside temperature between minus fifteen and twenty five °C was a highly stressing experience, even with electrically heated clothes and Dexedrine.

Their willingness was irreproachable, many of them were airsick during these long night flights but were not disclosing anything to doctors, like P/O Kenneth Bryan, afraid of being discharged from flying. Leslie Sutton was shot down during his first combat flight, he could have stopped flying but he flew thirty five "Ops" after that. he really deserved his DFC.

The same determination to fight Nazis existed in all the Allied Air Forces. US losses amounted to about 60,000 during WWII. These figures have to be compared with losses of Free French Air Forces, which were in the few hundreds. I don't want to open a controversial discussion, but simply put in perspective these sad figures for the French who criticise their American and English friends with words sometimes rather too extreme.

Those men and women gave their lives to defend our Freedom, we should always remember them. It is not unreasonable to say that, without their sacrifice, we would most probably all be speaking German today.

On the German side, it was worse, if I may say so. Airmen were showing the same eagerness to fight. The Luftwaffe rule was simple. you fly until you die. Eighty thousand planes were shot down during the war, resulting in one hundred and thirty thousand airmen being killed. Allied forces controlled German skies only in 1945, after the arrival of long range fighters like the P47, P51 and P38 which could defend and protect bombers all the way through.

At the end of war, after such heavy losses, the Luftwaffe was lacking in trained pilots. In 1945, they had a desperate project "Elbe", using almost unarmed fighters to hit bombers, but giving a chance for pilots to survive before hitting the enemy. This project had poor results and was classed as a failure overall.

Between fighters, rules close to chivalry applied. Opponents tried when they could to avoid killing the other, if not least helping them to return home. Numerous testimonies have been recorded. It has been mentioned in many reports that pilots, after the war, tried to contact the German pilot who shot them down. Unfortunately, in many cases they discovered he had been killed a few days later. There is no good war, we can never say this enough.

Strategic Bombing was much criticised during the Thirties. some even proposed to prohibit its use in international conflicts. The Germans were the first during WWI who implemented strategic bombing using Zeppelins, without notable success. However, the role played by the RAF Bomber Command and Sir Arthur Harris's firm management has been also criticised even though he had a strong support from Churchill, who called him "Bomber Harris". Critics say ultimately losses during the air raids over Germany at night and at high altitude remained very high but did not have a significant impact on the Nazis' morale. This was true because of the inaccuracy of the bombing. Many civilians were killed; an estimate of 600,000 has been suggested for Germany and 60,000 for France.

But Churchill wrote immediately after the Armistice in 1945, 'the contribution of Bomber Command had been decisive in the final defeat of Germany…" and the Lancaster greatly contributed to the implementation of this strategy.

After the war, William McGown, the "skipper" in our story, returned all his decorations to the RAF. I was given two reasons for his actions. The controversy mentioned above meant that Bomber Command did not receive at the end of the war proper recognition from the British Government. The other explanation is the revisionists' number of civilians killed in Germany.

I am not going to take a position on this issue. I'll just point out that Hitler first did the same thing and for the same reasons in 1940, during the Battle of Britain and then with the V1 and V2s, killing thousands of civilians in the United Kingdom.

I believe that Sir Arthur Harris and many others with him believed in the same strategy, like Churchill who supported him. The US did the same, with bombings in day at high altitude, even flying with tight formations and fighter protection. Returning flights were difficult to coordinate and protect because allied forces did not control the sky over Germany.

They did the best they could to deal with a real danger whose greatest horrors were only discovered at the end of the war. We should also mention the losses occurred at sea, 50,000 sailors in the Royal Navy, 36,000 sailors in the merchant fleets and some 5,000 ships sunk. We cannot rewrite history; it is too easy to say afterwards that it was a failure, sitting comfortably in a chair, without having to make a decision the next day.

An undeniable fact is recognised that these bombings still slowed the German war effort despite the tremendous development of the aerospace industry, ahead of the rest of the world in the areas of jet fighters, the V1 and V2 rockets, and research into nuclear weapons. It also slowed the supply of essential fuel to the movement of armies.

A major achievement of SOE, Special Operations Executive, was to destroy the stock of "heavy water" produced in Norway by Norsk Hydro with a few dozen elite Norwegian commandos trained in Scotland and parachuted at night near the plant in the mountain in Norway. Thanks to this victory, the stock was sunk in one of the deepest fjords in Norway and the production of an atomic bomb by Germany postponed by several months.

German scientists working on all new development projects were not obliged to go to war, a strong incentive for them not to lack motivation. They were all hired back at the end of war by the Allied countries eager for their expertise.

Last but not least, we should not forget the role played by the Underground during the war which helped shot down airmen by risking their lives to get them back to UK to continue fighting.

Chances of survival in a bomber shot down were less than one in the six, if we take the example of 514 Squadron. for about 80 bombers shot down on ops from a total of 163 aircraft used, 429 airmen were killed, 35 evaded and 34 became prisoners of war.

Those landing safely in France were all helped by local civilians at the beginning. One out of two was held prisoner afterwards, following betrayals, difficulty to stay hidden when you don't speak the language, and sometimes, it has to be said, for money given by the Gestapo[2]. This is what happened to John Clarke, Lyndon Lewis, Ken Chapman, Phil Lamason and many others.

Some airmen, eager to fight, even in occupied territories, participated in Underground resistance activities, like Lyndon Lewis, before being held prisoners. Many of them had been shot like the father of Andree de Jongh, or deported like the father of Josselyne Pichon, Andree de Jongh, Frantzia Usandisaga, Juan Larburu and Virginia d'Albert Lake. Many of them did not come back.

---

[2] Gestapo: Geheime Staatspolizei. German Secret State Police.

The Gestapo were offering a reward of ten thousand francs, about two thousand euros, to anyone who helped in the arrest of an airman. Posters displayed in town halls in 1941 advertised any man arrested helping airmen would be shot and any woman doing the same would be deported, which was not much better treatment.

This sanction was applied to Andrée de Jongh and her father, Frantzia Usandizaga and Juan Manuel Larburu in Basque country. Frantzia and Juan did not come back, nor did Josselyne Pichon's father. The 'Comet Line" history is exceptional in many aspects, bringing several hundred soldiers home to the UK during the war.

The Resistance also paid a heavy price during the war, there are no reliable statistics, but the figure of about one hundred thousand killed has been estimated by some historians, which seems a reasonable estimate. Andrée de Jongh used to say to newcomers in her group. 'The only question is not whether you will be arrested or not, but when? With me, you will last about six months on average.'

What is noticeable, when you speak to all those who were lucky enough to come back alive, they all say unanimously the same thing: "If I had to do it all again, I would". It is to be noted, however, that in the German concentration camps there were not only Resistance members. Sometimes people having collaborated with the enemy were also deported.

We have lost the trace of many of them like the father of Josselyne Lejeune-Pichon and Juan Larburu. These are wounds that will never fade in the memory of those who lived through these horrible times. There is no good war, we can never say that enough.

I would not end this preface without mentioning the names of Captain François de Labouchere and General Pierre Marie Gallois, two great heroes of WWII.

François started to fly in 1936 and joined the French Air Force in September 1939. He was a student in "Ecole de l'Air" (Flight School) at the time of the armistice. He went to Morocco to continue fighting. His father Pierre de Labouchere, commanding an armoured battalion belonging to the 6th Dragons Regiment, had been killed on June 5th on the battlefield in Cavillon (Somme). François learned of his death when he was boarding a ship in Bayonne leaving for Morocco, Gibraltar and England.

François de Labouchere (courtesy of Solange Marchal)

.He arrived in Liverpool, England, in July 1940. There were 22 French airmen who joined the RAF then (see Appendix 12), a few among those whom Churchill mentioned in a famous speech . "Never in the field of human conflict was so much owed by so many to so few". Sixteen of them, out of 22, did not come back.

A Spitfire pilot, he was part of the Battle of Britain in 1940, a decisive victory which prevented the invasion of Great Britain by the Germans. He had claimed several air victories and sank about twenty ships when his Spitfire BL 803 was shot down during a dog fight in the Somme bay against a group of Focke Wulf 190 which outnumbered them, on September 5th 1942. Francois and his three wing fellows V J Dubourgel (W3705), R A J Taconet (BM 400) et L B Thibaud (BL 854) were attacked from above with the sun at their back, they did not have any chance to escape.

He had been awarded the DFC just before in July 1942. He was appointed "Compagnon de la Libération" in January 1943, "Croix de Guerre" and "Légion d'Honneur". His body was never found. He had been flying wing to wing with his great friends Emile (François) Fayolle (killed two weeks before on 19th August 1942 in Dieppe) and the famous Group Captain Peter Townsend.

On several occasions I had met General Pierre Marie Gallois, the first time being in 1968. He was Navigator in a Halifax of RAF Bomber Command from 1943 to 1945. He made more than thirty combat missions

General P M Gallois in company of Serge Sireau (courtesy of Serge Sireau)

from Elvington in Yorkshire. He was then the great strategist of the French Nuclear Deterrent Force. In 1956 he had convinced the Socialist Guy Mollet, then General de Gaulle, to set up the French Strategic Nuclear Air Force with the supersonic Mach 2.2 Dassault Mirage IV bomber.

In the Sixties, he was having lunch once a month with Marcel Dassault and General Lecamus, then at the head of DTCA[3] I had asked General Gallois to preface this book, he answered me back a few weeks before passing away. "At my age (about 100) I only write scrawls." I keep his letter carefully in a safe place.

This was a real loss for our story. Having flown in Halifax bombers in RAF Bomber Command from 1943 to 1945, we could not have had a better witness or testimony for the Preface. After the war, he had really been the great thinker of the French Nuclear "Dissuasion" Strategy. "Have the Nuclear power yourself to dissuade the enemy from using it."

In the Fifties, during the Cold war, having realised a nuclear bomb and a few men had been able to put an end to a world conflict which killed

---

[3] DTCA: Direction Technique des Constructions de l'Aéronautique (French Air Technical Department) who supervised all aerospace projects in France, including Concorde.

fifty million people, he convinced the French Government to implement the Nuclear Programme utilising the Mirage IV as means of delivery, before missiles were operational, and he fought constantly for peace in the world throughout his life.

The Mirage IV would need to be refuelled in the air by US KC 135 jet tankers (military tanker variant of Boeing 707) in order to have enough range to reach the Soviet Union. Pilots were trained above the North Pole. Fifteen KC 135 had been bought by France from the USA in the sixties to support the project; without them pilots striking the USSR would have had a "one way ticket".

Anti-aircraft missiles made some progress in the meantime; initial plans were to drop the nuclear bomb from an altitude of 65,000 ft. In a second phase the Mirage IVs were supposed to drop their bombs at a low altitude under the radar coverage.

May his memory be honoured as one of the RAF fellows of Bomber Command.

Introduction

This following story is true and is the direct result of a great and beautiful friendship, woven over time within a small group of people who did not know each other at the outset, the "Lancaster family", as it is called now. These people shared a love of the legendary Lancaster bomber shot down sixty years ago in the Chevreuse valley, above my native village La Celle-les-Bordes. Thanks to this family of friends this story has been patiently restored day after day for the past 70 years.

All the facts presented are true. We have compared testimonies from the people involved as well as direct friends and family about the same event whenever we could; however memories after sixty years sometimes lack accuracy.

As we will see, the story was born out of a coming together between a child and a plane which fell from the sky; I cannot really say I chose it. By a number of sometimes surprising coincidences they allowed us to find a number of people involved at the time, some of whom are still alive to day. In doing so, we discovered facts within our little group without originally being fully aware of them.

History is a great story. As you will see, it accurately describes what happened on the ground and shows the courage and tenacity of those involved when confronted with real difficulties during really troubled times. Chance and everybody's natural instinct to help certainly explain why we were so successful in our research.

The strong link established within "The Lancaster family" also sparked numerous meetings and has helped to find many of the people involved such as those who lived near the area during 1944 or those who directly helped to contribute at the time. the extraordinary list has John Tanney and and Leslie Sutton in England both aged 90, Ydoine Riviere in France aged 89, Neil Bryan in Australia aged 84 and Phillip Lamason in New Zealand aged 93 to name but a few.

As a result, the story inevitably involves the families' stories and those who intervened on the ground, the last being Les Sutton and Ed Greenburgh plus two American families. The Lancaster brought me back to my childhood roots and thanks to her I found friends from when I was young.

Our meetings are always warm and memories come back as if time had stopped.

It has also made me rediscover the life of my native village, the life of my parents and my close friends during the war, as official archives such as the Register of Civil Status are not really romantic, whilst MI9 British Secret Military reports were only distributed to the families or next of kin.

The aid and research from government authorities has been remarkable and invaluable. We also need to thank Mayor Serge Querard, Colonel Alain Populaire and the French Air Force in Velizy, the English Embassy in Paris, Révérend Philip Mountstephen from St Michael's in Paris, Father F Coeur from St Arnoult, without forgetting the Carnutes Choir and Sergeant Piper Lopez who came paying a tribute to Scottish airmen near their memorial in the forest in November 2009.

We have found all the way through that everybody has volunteered to help, without forgetting the primary school classmates of my native village, La Celle-les-Bordes and the Mayor who so ably assisted in getting in touch with all those searching for the same facts. Jean Huon, Roger Guernon, Kenneth Wright, Sinclair Ronald and Stan Kershaw

Surprising as it may seem, we all lived a happy childhood during the war in La Celle-les-Bordes, even though times were really troubled in an otherwise occupied country. We did not face too many violent fights in the village and had only one soldier killed in 1940, Atman Raba from Algeria, when the Germans invaded France.

Children have a natural tendency to only retain good memories. The typical noise of the Merlin or Hercules engines flying above our houses, aluminium strips dropped by the bombers overhead to confuse the enemy radars all of which were really part of my childhood and remain etched in my memory. Maybe that is the reason why I later went to work in aviation. It is clear however my childhood was influenced by many planes flying overhead. We as children of La Celle-les-Bordes, are really a singular group that worships the village much like the villagers in the stories of Asterix did theirs. Did we, perhaps, fall in a cauldron of magical potion? This does not fail to annoy our spouses or husbands as not everyone has the chance to keep such a strong attachment to the place of their childhood.

The children of La Celle in the valley were constantly fighting like cats with the children from les-Bordes in the fields. We were really two distinct groups. When the fighting ended, we were all solid friends. Many of us say the same thing, these years were for us among the best in our lives.

In the early fifties, many airmen who had been shot down in the area and survived the war came back to their escape route. This also sparks another great memory for me, like that of the Lancaster as I was impressed they were all speaking English.

On many occasions, I found places or facts directly linked to the history of the Lancaster which were very close to my own life only from discussions I had with my mother. Quite often I was told that people could not remember anything about what was said and that it was probably made up. The so called "Countess of Montenegro" is the best example of this. Her daughter Geraldine was found thanks to my childhood friend "Pussy", Anne-Marie Sanderson, who only remembered her first name "Anne-Marie" and Josselyne Lejeune-Pichon. I remember my two brothers laughing at me as if she was purely in my imagination. The first time I spoke to Geraldine she asked. "Where and how did you find Montenegro?"

There are dozens of these coincidences as you will discover through the course of history. The life of ordinary people often hides adventure and romance. I did not choose, "the story fell on my head" as I say sometimes, just like the Lancaster falling from the sky. On several occasions, I had the spiritual sensation that I had been guided. You will discover these coincidences when we progress.

The 70th anniversary of D-Day was commemorated in France on June 6th, 2014 with the presence of twenty heads of state who came to Normandy from all over the world, representing effectively all the heroes of our story. It is important to keep alive the memory of what happened then, a time will come when all surviving veterans and their testimonies will be gone. The effective participation of twenty countries[4] to celebrations is comforting and brings hope for the future of Peace and Freedom in the world.

So please enjoy the flight with us.

Francois Ydier, Plaisir, March 2016

---

[4] Australia, Belgium, Canada, Czech Republic, Germany, Greece, Italy, Luxemburg, Monaco, Netherlands, New Zealand, Norway, Poland, Russian Federation, Ukraine, United Kingdom, United States.

Monday June 5th, 1944

The eve of the full moon. Pilot Officers William McGown and Lyndon Warwick Lewis flew with the rest of their crew to bomb the German coastal defences of the Atlantic wall in the vicinity of Ouistreham. Their aircraft was an Avro Lancaster Mk.II, serial number LL620, of 514 Squadron based at Waterbeach near Cambridge in England. 22 aircraft from 514 Squadron were detailed to bomb the primary target at Ouistreham.

Lyndon Lewis, the Bomb Aimer, said. "We left at 03.45 am. From my position at the front of the plane I could clearly see what was happening in front of me. Our mission, if I may say so, was an easy one. Only a three hour flight, round trip. We were flying at a low altitude, only 9,000 ft in a protected area on most of the trip and the bombing altitude was around 5/6,000 ft.

At day break, at around 05.15 am, when we were on our way back, I saw on the port side one of the most extraordinary scenes I had ever witnessed in my entire life, a formidable armada of seven thousand ships lined up over dozens of miles all along the English coast.

Immediately, I knew what was coming and I told my skipper and others on the intercom. D-Day has arrived, they are about to land on Normandy beaches. The secret had been kept until the last minute. The landing initially scheduled on June 5th, had been postponed because of bad weather which developed in the Channel on Saturday June 3rd.

At last, we could see the end to a deadly conflict in which we had fought for the past four years. We returned to Waterbeach at around 06.00 am. Without knowing it, we had just prepared for the landing of Allied troops for the next morning…" In the evening of June 5th, the first 82nd Airborne US division paratroopers arrived in the south of Cherbourg to place markers on the landing fields.

D-Day - Tuesday June 6th, 1944

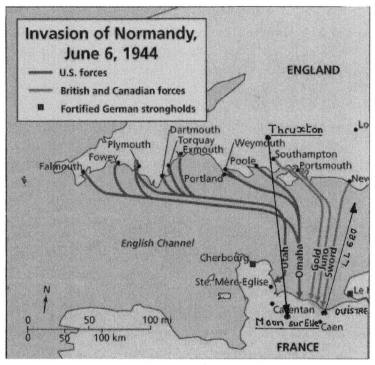

An overview of Overlord: the routes taken by the invasion fleet across the English Channel.

General Dwight D Eisenhower, after a thorough analysis, decided to launch the landing on Normandy coast for Tuesday June 6th. The weather was not that great, but having deciphered German secret messages, they knew Hitler and Rommel were convinced they would land in the Pas de Calais area.

The night before, with his fellows from the 82nd Airborne US division, Pierre Schumann (who had been given the pseudonym *Saville* in 1939) had landed in the area of Ste Mere-Eglise.

At around 7.00 am, as everywhere along Normandy beaches, thirty thousand soldiers landed in the sector of Sword Beach, near Ouistreham. Allied troops coming from Portsmouth, along with S Task Force (for Sword), the first Special Services brigade comprising 1850 men split over seven elite

2nd Lt William J McGowan, courtesy Paul Stouffer.

Commando units[5], landed at around 7 . 30 am. It was headed by General Simon Fraser, the 15th Lord Lovat.

In the "Queen Red Sector", on the left side of Sword Beach, Lord Lovat, against the rules, ordered William "Bill" Pepill to pipe the men ashore whilst under fire. Germans, watching him come ashore, did not shoot as they thought he was completely crazy.

The only two French commandos units present that day (out of 177 commandos in total) were directed by the Colonel Phillipe Kieffer. They had been added to the Special Services brigade and, by courtesy, were the first to land on the French soil. The day before, when D DAY was announced, Lovat told them in French "*Nous allons avoir la peau des Boches.*" (We are going to kill the "Boches").

A coincidence in history: the No. 1 Commando was directed by the Captain Guy Vourc'h, the cousin of a classmate in Nantes Lycee, Joël Vourc'h. His family was well represented that day, another parent, Lieutenant Francis Vourc'h was also fighting with No. 8 Commando. They both survived the war.

The overall objective assigned to Colonel Kieffer and his commando units was to neutralise Riva Bella and the Ouistreham casino near the coast line. Philippe had declared to his men who had all followed the hard physical and mental 'Green Berets' training reserved for elite troops in Achnacarry camp in Scotland, "We will not all return". At 09.30 am, they had reached

---

[5] Commandos Nos. 3, 4, 6, 45 (1st Service Brigade)   1, 8 (French, Colonel P Kieffer) 10 (Other Allied forces)

their first objective. 21 of them were killed that day, 93 were injured, including Colonel Kieffer, who was himself wounded twice.

Lovat's objective was to take the control of Ouistreham harbour and Benouville Bridge (later renamed Pegasus Bridge). He took control at 12.02 and met with the paratroopers who had landed nearby overnight. When he arrived he said "I apologise, we were two minutes behind the plan."

2nd Lt William Joseph McGowan, 23, was born in Benson, Minnesota. He had graduated six months before with W J Buttner from the P47 advanced pilot training school of Harding Field, Baton Rouge, Louisiana. Whilst there, he had married Suzanne Schaeffer on February 15th 1944, before being sent overseas in England in April to the 366th Fighter Bomber Group of the US 9th Air Force. His group was tasked with strafing German convoys.

On Tuesday, June 6th, 1944, William came to Normandy to meet his destiny. It was his third combat mission of the day, providing tactical support to the D Day landings. In total more than 10,000 planes were sent to the Normandy coast. William was searching with five other P47s for "*Razorback*" a railway convoy transporting equipment which had been spotteded in the St. Lo area. For easy identification, black and white stripes were painted on the fuselage and wings of Allied aircraft, with the exception of heavy bombers. He took off at around 16.00 pm from Thruxton in England – a thirty minutes flight from the Normandy coast line – to attack the convoy. Thruxton was an airfield jointly utilised by RAF and USAAF, particularly for gliders towed by C-47 Dakotas (the military version of the DC-3) for transporting troops to the Normandy coast.

Having failed to find the train, the group of fighters decided to attack Lison railway station. William was hit by Flak[6] during the attack before being able to drop his bomb. He was flying at low altitude, at about 500 ft. His engine was set on fire. The aircraft stalled whilst climbing and making a U-turn. William crashed with his plane in Moon Sur Elle county; however he still took great care to avoid hitting the church and neighbouring castle.

According to the testimony of his comrade F/O Paul E Strycker and evidence gathered on the ground, the crash resulted in an enormous

---

[6] FLAK: German FL (ieger) A (bwerh) K(anone), anti-aircraft guns. Shells did not hit the planes directly, they were calibrated to explode after a predetermined time.

explosion and fire that lasted several hours. His five other colleagues paid him a tribute by flying over the burning wreck whose engine was stuck deep in the ground. They then went on to destroy the FLAK batteries nearby which had killed William, before flying back to Thruxton.

11,590 planes had been engaged in combat that day. 10,500 Allied soldiers were killed, about the same number on the German side. By comparison, civilian casualties resulting from bombings and combats during the entire Normandy campaign came up about 20,000.

The Germans were about to lose the war, they had been misled by the absolute secret prevailing around the *Overlord* operation and the disinformation sown that said the landing would be held in Pas de Calais. The troops sent to reinforce German defences arrived in Normandy too late. This had been essential for a successful attack, but was not guaranteed. Even though everything had been cautiously planned and organised, General Dwight D Eisenhower had prepared a statement saying he himself bore the responsibility in the case Allied armies had suffered a defeat.

That day Bob Maloubier, a secret agent of SOE section F[7] had participated in a guerilla operation in the Limoges area. He was only informed after his return to England in the evening that the landing had begun in Normandy in the morning.

---

[7] SOE "Special Operations Executive" English Secret Service created by Churchill in July 1940

A Fateful Night. June 7-8th, 1944

We were living in La Celle-les-Bordes Town Hall and School, which was built on a hillside in the forest between the two villages of La Celle in the valley and Les-Bordes on the plateau. This is where I was born in late 1942, just between Rambouillet and Chevreuse.

My mother was extremely happy when D-Day was announced and it was like she had regained her pride previously lost, as she used to say, when Marshal Petain stopped the fighting during June 1940 and declared Paris to be an open city. I was about 18 months old at the time. Everybody had been waiting for the invasion for months, but nobody knew where and when it would be.

RAF Bomber Command's mission during the night of June 7th – 8th was to provide tactical support by bombing communications targets. The objective was to cut off all roads, bridges and railway tracks in the Paris region that might allowing German troops to reach the Normandy front. 337 bombers left England at night from 17 different English airfields between 10.00 pm and 01.00 am.

The village was just starting to fall asleep, when the hordes of Halifax and Lancaster bombers were heard arriving over the Chevreuse Valley in successive waves at around 23.00 hrs. There was an average of about one plane every 30 seconds. It was impossible to sleep due to the bellowing noise of the distinctive Merlin and Hercules engines, the echoes of which caused vibrations of the house windows. You could see the sky was full of aircraft flying in all directions, followed by flak and the searchlight beams in Rambouillet and Limours coning the aircraft up to 6,000 ft high.

The explosions of flak shells and German night fighters' tracer were adding to the Dante-esque scene. Now and then, a bomber would be shot down, the engine note changing followed by a huge explosion as the aircraft crashed to its fatal end on the ground.

The objectives of the RAF bombing were mainly targets in the South and West of Paris. They were concentrated in five areas; Acheres, Versailles, Chevreuse, Juvisy and Massy Palaiseau.

La Celle-les-Bordes was located on the route of most bombers attacking or returning to England, which were preceded by about thirty aircraft placing markers on the targets, using colour-coded flares.

In total seventeen Lancaster's and fifteen Halifax's crashed during that fateful night; twenty six in the Paris area, two in Normandy and four severely damaged above France which managed to return to England. One Mk. III Halifax of 158 Squadron had also crashed during take-off in Lissett, fortunately without any reported casualties.

The rate of losses recorded that night was among one of the highest for Bomber Command at that stage of the war. In another MkIII Halifax from 429 Squadron, S/L. W.B. Anderson was mortally wounded by flak over the Dieppe area. He gave his final order for his fellow airmen to abandon the plane before he died. Three of them baled out. Sergeant G.E.J. Steere then took the controls and succeeded in bringing back the plane near to Benson in England with his critically injured skipper attached to a static line.

One hundred and forty five airmen died during that fateful night, out of a total of two hundred and twenty eight aircrew in the aircraft shot down. Among them, three unfortunately died after their return to England in their badly damaged aircrafts.

The table in Appendix 6 gives a detailed breakdown by nationality of each crew member and their precise fate. From June 6, attacks were penetrating further and further into French territory. Aircraft started flying at lower altitudes to make accurate bombing attacks minimizing civilian losses; however this increased their risk of being shot down.

This also gave more time for the German night fighters to attack them. All they had to do was just wait for them to pass overhead. They would shoot from below in an infernal attack procedure called "Schräge Musik" *(Vertical firing cannon mounted to the fuselage of some German night fighters)*. This technique sometimes caused the bomber to hit the German night fighters once they had been shot down.

P/O I.V. 'Pop' Seddon, 26, from Australia had taken off from Lissett on Thursday June 8th at 00.06 am in a Halifax MkIII (a). His target was the marshalling yards at Versailles. His aircraft was hit at around 01.30 am by flak and a night fighter near Rambouillet during his approach to the target.

With his port wing set afire, Pop gave the order to abandon the plane. The entire crew baled out, five, including Pop, through the forward exit hatch at 6,000 ft and two through the rear exit door at 4,500 ft. They all landed safely in the Rambouillet area. The Halifax went a further 12 miles south and crashed near Allainville with her full bomb load.

The German squadron leader Walter Borchers, a 28 year old German ace with 22 claimed victories, had taken off from Athies-Laon to the north of Paris at around 01.00 am. He was flying a twin-engined Messerchmitt BF110 equipped with deadly dorsal *'Shräge Musik'* guns shooting upwards. Walter was flying with a navigator and a gunner. He patrolled in the area at a constant altitude of four thousand feet, waiting for the passage of bombers flying above him in their descent to target or returning home to England. In his log book, Walter states that he shot down three bombers in ten minutes (see Appendix 7) on that day raising his number of victories to twenty five.

514 Squadron based at Waterbeach had deployed fourteen aircraft on this operation. Unfortunately two MkII Lancasters did not return (b).

The first was LL727 A2-C. She had taken off at 00.27 am, her target being Massy Palaiseau marshalling yards. She had a crew of eight; the pilot F/O. Louis "Lou" Greenburgh DFC, aged 28, was Canadian and his co-pilot W/O. Leslie Sutton, aged 22 was on his 'second dickey' operational experience flight. The skipper despite being a Canadian national had joined the RAF directly, rather than the RCAF.

   (a) Lissett - 158 Squadron - Halifax III - LL863 NP-C
       Target   Versailles
       T/O   00H06   Pilot - P/O I.V. Seddon, RAAF

   (b) Waterbeach - 514 Squadron - LL727 A2-C Lancaster MKII
       Target - Massy Palaiseau
       T/O   00H27   Pilot - F/O. L. Greenburgh RAF

       DS822 JI-T Lancaster MKII
       Target - Villeneuve St.Georges
       T/O   00H37   Pilot - P/O W.L. McGown RAF

Gordon Stromberg	Leslie Weddle		Fred Carey	Pat Butler
W/Op	F/E		M/U/G	Nav
	Colin Drake	Lou Greenburgh	Don Bament	
	R/G	Pilot	B/A	

F/O Lou Greenburgh DFC and his original crew (courtesy of Ed Greenburgh).

The second Lancaster MKII was DS822 JI-T, she took off ten minutes later at 00.37 am. Her target was Villeneuve St. Georges marshalling yards, located 6 miles East from Massy.

LL727 was attacked once by a night fighter just before reaching her goal at around 01.55 am. Louis was in the final approach to their target. Despite the attack Louis successfully dropped his bomb load and then gave the order to abandon the plane. The co-pilot W/O Leslie Sutton, F/S Bomb Aimer Eric G Rippingale, F/Sgt Engineer F Collingwood F/Sgt R Fox jumped out and landed in Saulx Les Chartreux County, near Orly[8].

The following report is supplied by courtesy of Ed Greenburgh.

---

[8] The original crew had been rescued after ditching in the North Sea on 29/30th December 1943. On 24/25th March 1944, the crew was badly shot up returning from Berlin. Greenburgh ordered them to bale out and Weddle, Butler and Bayment had done so when Butler told Greenburgh he had lost his parachute. Greenburgh, Stromberg, Carey and Drake managed to get their crippled aircraft home. Drake left the crew in early May 1944. Stromberg and Carey were with Greenburgh when they were shot down on 7/8th June 1944.

Squadron Leader Phillip Lamason RNZAF, DFC and his crew were also shot down on the Massy Palaiseau raid. Lamason would feature later in the story (Crown copyright).

Seeing his plane had not been badly damaged during the first attack, Lou decided then to pursue his return flight, probably flying above Paris. He was attacked later by the Junker 88 of Hauptmann Herbert Lorenz and was shot down at 02H55 above St-Eusoye, 20 kilometers North East of Beauvais.

The four airmen left on board baled out then. Sgt. F.J. Carey MU Gunner, the Wireless Operator F/S G.H. Stromberg, Sgt. R.S. Woosnam the Rear Gunner, the pilot F/O. L. Greenburgh DFC. The Wireless Operator, "Strommy" aged 19, was badly hurt in landing on an electrical line. Even though he was cautiously taken down by Germans and transported to Amiens hospital, he died two days later.

The first Lancaster shot down by Walter Borchers could be the one that crashed in Tacoignieres, MKIII LM491 GI-E (c) from 622 Squadron who had taken off at Mildenhall, at 00.35 am and was part of the Massy Palaiseau group. She is the one whom Josselyne Lejeune-Pichon wrote about. She was in descent on her way to her target when she was shot down at 02.21 am. Another explosion in the night which made a huge hole in the ground and broke many windows around the crash area. The airmen did not

Major Walter Borchers claimed three Lancasters on the Massy Palaiseau raid. It is believed that he shot down DS822. Borchers himself was killed on 5/6th March 1945 when he was shot down by an RAF Mosquito (courtesy of 514 Squadron Society).

have the time to abandon the plane, causing them all to perish in the crash. They are all buried in Tacoignieres cemetery.

The Lancaster LM575 MKIII had taken off from Mildenhall at 00.42 am (c) and was also part of the Massy Palaiseau group. She was shot down above Plaisir at 02.29 am. Her skipper was S/L. Phillip Lamason, aged 25, from the Royal New Zealand Air Force. His target was Trappes marshalling yards.

Lamason arrived on target before markers had been placed. The lighting missiles Target Markers placed normally in advance by other PPF aircraft, of which their colour had been confirmed during the briefing for each target. Instead of coming back with his bomb load, only to have had to drop it above the channel to be able to land safely in UK, Phillip decided to return to his target a second time, flying at 7,500 ft to stay above Flak range.

It was then that Lieutenant (Oberleutnant) Walter Borchers who was patrolling below at 4,000 ft started shooting at his plane. Phillip engaged the combat with the night fighter but an incendiary shell set afire his starboard wing (see Appendix 7, W. Borchers claimed victories).

(c)   Mildenhall
      Squadron 15 -   Lancaster MKIII - LM575, LS-H
      Target - Trappes
      T/O - 00H42   Pilot - S/L. P.J. Lamason   RNZAF

Squadron 622 - Lancaster MkIII LM491, GI-E
Target - Massy Palaiseau
T/O - 00H35   Pilot   P/O J.E. Hall   RAF

Phillip then gave the order to evacuate the plane. During the fight, the Lancaster had lost a lot of altitude. The crew were forced to bale out low. Phillip pushed out his Navigator, "Chappy". The two gunners were unfortunately killed. The Rear Gunner, F/O. T. W. Dunk, RAF from Bulawayo Rhodesia, stayed in the rear turret shooting until the end. The parachute of W/O. R.B. Aitken, RAF, from Scotland, opened too late. During his parachute descent, Phillip saw the starboard wing breaking from the aircraft causing it to drop out of the sky like a stone.

The third Lancaster (b) shot down by Walter at 02.31 am could be the Lancaster MKII, DS822, JI-T flown by P/O William McGown from 514 Squadron.

The Luftwaffe claims having shot down thirty bombers during the night between 01.04 am and 03.12 am. This sad figure is strictly in line with losses declared by RAF Bomber Command.

Monique Dacheux, who was eight years old at the time and was living just next door to the Château des Bordes, occupied temporarily by German soldiers rushing to the Normandy beaches. At around 02.00 am, Monique's family was awakened by her father. After seeing and hearing what was happening outside, he decided to bring everybody in the shelter he had built at the end of their garden a few hundred yards from the house.

In such a case, each child had a specific task. Monique was supposed to take a bag containing official family papers. In the haste, she forgot it that night. When arriving to the shelter, her father asked her to return to collect it.

It was at this time when walking back home at about approximately 02.30 am that she saw an aircraft in flames flying above her head. It was Lancaster DS822 JI-T, with two engines on fire. The pilot, P/O William McGown was about to abandon the plane as he was the last one to do so, which she could not see in the darkness of the night.

A few minutes earlier, coming back from having bombed her target, Villeneuve St.Georges, the plane had first been hit by flak shells and then by a night fighter piloted by Walter Borchers. With two engines in flames, the

The Boy and the Bomber

A line-up of MkII Lancasters at Waterbeach in January 1944. The Bristol Hercules engines make a significant difference to the appearance of the aircraft, most of which were powered by the more familiar Rolls-Royce Merlin (courtesy of 514 Squadron Society).

aircraft could have had exploded at any time. P/O William McGown, 31, gave the order to abandon the plane when arriving above Bonnelles (see return flight map page **57**).

He was the last to abandon the plane through the fore exit door located right below the post of Bomb Aimer. The plane was flying at 6,000 ft, heading now North West, with autopilot "On" to keep the plane horizontal and get out in good conditions.

The three other airmen in the front part "Jack" A.N. Durham, Navigator, F/S John Clarke Engineer and P/O Lyndon Lewis Bomb aimer, baled out in that order using the same emergency exit that Lyndon had opened in simply throwing out the hatch. They all landed safely.

William and his three team mates did not know what the three others had done in the rear. W/O. Ken Bryan W/Op. who went there to check the status of the tail hit by Flak, F/Sgt. George Boanson, M.U. Gunner and F/Sgt. Robert C. Guy Rear Gunner. W/O. Jack Durham landed near Bonnelles, two miles West of Longchene.

F/Sgt. John Clarke landed near Moutiers, he saw his plane crashing during his descent in the parachute which lasted about five minutes, a brief quiet moment in time, out of nowhere was the crackle of machine guns

Avro Lancaster MKII DS822, JI-T and her crew. They were serving with 514 Squadron, flying from RAF Waterbeach, near Cambridge. Boanson, Bryan and Guy are buried in La Celle-Les-Bordes (courtesy of Roger Guernon).

bullets on the frame, the noise of engines and flames spreading out into the fuselage.

The airmen did not receive much training for parachuting out of a plane, the instructions were to count up to ten to give some distance from the plane before opening to prevent snagging and tearing from the plane as encountered by F/S John Tanney, the predecessor of F/Sgt. Robert Guy. In the dark, P/O Lyndon Lewis afraid of opening too low, stopped counting at 5. He landed between two woods, near Les-Bordes, where Monique was living.

P/O William McGown landed a little further North, on plateau des Bordes, in the direction of Auffargis. German soldiers who had also seen the plane in flames, shot at him during his parachute descent, but thankfully missed.

DS822 Lancaster left alone with Autopilot "On", continued her flight. She began turning left and engaged in a spin. After two or three turns, the fuselage broke up, right before the rear exit door which had probably been opened by Ken or George in the rear, whilst getting prepared to bail out.

F/S Robert Guy, was trapped in the rear turret and fell with the tail. W/O. Ken Bryan and F/S George Boanson were thrown out when the plane broke in two. It is practically impossible to exit a plane whilst spinning, because of the G forces (acceleration).

Their bodies were found severely burned in "the Little Forest", ("la Petite Forêt") with their parachutes not opened. They had most probably been killed during the attack of the German night fighter.

At Waterbeach, the plane has been registered MIA - "Missing in Action" on June 8th at around 6.30 am. Her flight plan indicated a return to base at around 3.15 am with a fuel reserve of about three hours.

Thursday June 8th in the morning, Johnny Boule, aged 15, was walking in the forest. He was at a distance of about two miles from his home in Les-Bordes and was probably the first to witness the wreck, except maybe woodcutters working in the forest.

Johnny found the tail quite intact on the ground among trees with F/Sgt. Robert Guy's body near-by. There was no trace of fire around, however masses of debris and machines gun ammunition sprawled from three turrets. Seeing this, Johnny immediately ran back, as he knew the Germans forbade anyone from touching anything that had fallen from the sky. On his way back home, in "Bois des Gaules", he met a group of German soldiers who arrested him, asking him if he had seen something.

Johnny knew perfectly well what the Germans were looking for, the wreck but also surviving airmen. He said he was returning home to les-Bordes and had not seen anything or anybody. He was eventually released and ran away back home after having had the greatest fright of his young life.

Friday 9th June 1944

Anne Marie Errembault de Dudzeele (courtesy of Geraldine Cerf de Dudzeele).

The following morning, F/S John Clarke who had landed near Moutiers, had received food, civilian clothes and spent the night on a farm near Bullion. He met a young English speaking lady who arrived on a bicycle with a dog. She spoke English to him for a while, to check his identity (source MI9 – F. Prompsaud), because the Germans were trying to infiltrate the Underground networks. She said to John, I'll come back to pick you up tomorrow morning and we will go to Chevreuse.

Following her route, Anne-Marie went to Poigny la Foret, near Rambouillet to meet the crew of the Australian skipper P/O I.V. "Pop" Seddon (Halifax III) who had crashed near Allainville on June 8th. Their presence had been reported to her by the Comet Line. in only one night, June 7-8, about fifty airmen survived landing in the Chevreuse valley…

Five airmen of the crew had been gathered by two local Resistance groups in a room on the first floor of the Hotel Restaurant "Au Petit Paris" owned by Mr. and Mrs. Bie in Poigny La Foret. A convenient location for airmen, as it was located outside the village to the corner of two roads at the junction of the D108 and D 936 heading to Rambouillet.

The Hostel was managed by Mrs. Angélique Bie, who had previously hidden several other airmen. Anne-Marie knew her very well, on several occasions she had spent the night there, when it was too late for her to come back home in St Remy Les Chevreuse, about fifteen miles in the forest.

Anne-Marie joined the airmen during the day. After having a short discussion with the two Resistance groups she went to discuss with the Halifax airmen in English. She said she could not do more for them than the others and that the other group would continue to arrange their escape. The Canadian F/O. Bill Leishman, who spoke a little French describes their meeting as follows in the story "Behind Enemy Lines".

"A quite pretty girl arrived then, well dressed with a sweater and a bag on her shoulder. She discussed for a while with two other groups of Resistants. She came to see us and said in English. 'I can't do more for you than the others, they will continue to take care of you and will help you to arrange your escape.' She had one brown eye and one blue eye. I will never forget how efficient she was, she had a revolver and had already killed a German soldier.

The inn "Au Petit Paris" Poigny La Foret in 1944 (courtesy of Christiane Leteissier).

A few German soldiers were having a drink in the café located on the ground floor. The group of airmen was in the room just above, they waited to leave the auberge until after all the Germans had left.

It was quite a busy day for "Antoinette" who had fifteen more miles to ride in the forest with her fox-terrier "Jimmy" to get back home. Her short meeting with F/O. Bill Leishman had been enough for him to understand Anne-Marie was an exceptional lady, 'a true "Calamity Jane" in the Chevreuse valley'.

I understand better now why my mother spoke of her with admiration, saying she surpassed all persons that she met in helping the airmen to escape during the war, exceeding all others with her guts. I have not invented the story, even though I didn't have any proof except what my mother was saying. I am happy and proud to pay Anne-Marie a tribute for what she did during the war. We have to remember her also.

Facts speak for themselves and her identification leaves now no room for error. You do not invent a Countess of Montenegro, with one blue eye and one brown eye, as we will see later.

Jean Louis Riviere, was living in Clairefontaine with his parents, having just been married to Ydoine. He was working in Paris during the week and was coming back Friday afternoons by train to Rambouillet. To this end, he left his bike near the station for the return journey back to Clairefontaine.

On Friday June 9th in the afternoon, cycling back home from the train station in Rambouillet, he saw a fire in the forest on his left. He said in arriving to his spouse Ydoine, 21 years old, a plane surely fell down in the forest, setting off a fire, we'll try to find it tomorrow, we can assume some of the airmen are seeking assistance and refuge in the forest.

Saturday June 10, 1944 – The Angel of Clairfontaine

Anne-Marie bicycle and her Fox Terrier "Jimmy" the dog on the left (courtesy of Géraldine Cerf de Dudzeele).

Anne-Marie Errembault de Dudzeele was aged 22, we know now that it was she who came back to take John Clarke as promised, near Bullion. The meeting had been arranged one mile from the farm where John had spent the night (Source MI9).

Anne-Marie placed her fox terrier "Jimmy" in a basket on the front of John's bicycle to distract the attention from him and avoid John speaking. The airmen were all declared dumb and not allowed to talk. Jimmy would bark every time he saw a German uniform approaching. John did not like dogs too much until this point and changed his mind afterwards. (Source HRH Daisy Clarke).

Taking small country roads they approached Chevreuse through Choisel, before finishing the trip through the road to Paris, the RD 906, for about one mile. The road was full of German convoys rushing to Normandy beaches.

We are now almost sure (see FFL certificate, Appendix 4) that she led John to the Kalmanson's home, in Chevreuse, a large house five hundred yards from Moulin des Clayes where Anne-Marie was living with her parents.

W/O. Archibald (Jack) N. Durham RAAF remained hidden on the farm of Guillaume Main. Due to transcription errors of the names from the archives found, we are uncertain as to the true name, it was either Mr Guillaume Main or Mr Marcel Guillaumain. We apologise in advance for families, but we have not been able to confirm the name of John's courageous host, as without any doubt, both have existed.

P/O Lyndon Lewis had begun walking in the direction of Paris. He had spent the night at the farm where he was given civilian clothes. P/O William McGowan had also been given a change of civilian clothes as well as something to eat. He continued in the direction of Paris, after having spent the night in the forest, out in the open.

On Saturday June 10th, Ydoine and Jean Louis Riviere went cycling in the morning in the same direction, where, the day before Jean Louis had seen a fire in the forest. They took the D72 heading to "La Villeneuve" then to "La Celle". They arrived in the valley and then took the D61 in the direction of La Noue farm and the D906. Climbing the hill, Jean Louis and Ydoine met woodcutters working there. They mentioned the plane, saying she crashed the night before, at around 02.00 am. They had found the bodies of F/S Robert Guy and W/O. Ken Bryan. German soldiers who had arrested Johnny had found and guarded the tail of the Lancaster in the morning but they still had not done anything for the airmen. The woodcutters did not want to touch anything as they were afraid of German reprisals.

Jean Louis and Ydoine Riviere, deeply shocked to see nothing had been done by Germans for the bodies of the airmen, decided then to give them a decent burial in the forest. The woodcutters made wooden crosses; Ydoine gathered a few flowers and they were both buried. The graves had almost been completed when a German officer arrived by car along the D61. The officer was quite an old man style. He stopped and asked them what they were doing. Jean Louis gave him the name of Ken Bryan found on his dog tag by the woodcutters. The German officer saluted the graves and then took a few notes on the identification numbers found on the plane frame. Graves were almost finished when the officer returned. He then saluted the graves one more time then clicked his heels and left the place without saying a single word.

When returning to Clairefontaine, Ydoine and Jean Louis went to see the priest, Father Fidèle Gallazini who was also in charge of La Celle-les-Bordes, and kept him informed of what they had done. They asked him to request from Kommandantur in Rambouillet authorisation to bury airmen in the La Celle cemetery, which he did right away leaving on his "Motobecane 125" motorbike. Father Gallazini belonged to the same underground network as my parents, unbeknown to the Riviere's.

This is how and why, Australian families and Kenneth Wright dubbed Ydoine Riviere the "Angel of Clairefontaine".

Around the same time, near Limoges, Nazi barbarism was unleashed with an SS Division rushing back from the South West to the Normandy Front. They had already sustained attacks from the Resistance the days before. The SS exterminated the entire village of Oradour Sur Glane (642 victims) in the afternoon even though the village had not engaged in violent action against the Germans before.

This barbaric act has never been clearly explained. Confusion could have been with the name of another Oradour village in the area, or as retaliation following the interception by a group of "Maquis" for the attack of a train transporting 600 kg of gold??? We will never know for sure, as the Germans could have simply understood they were starting to lose the war.

Funerals on Sunday June 11th

The next morning, the funerals of W/O. Ken Bryan and F/S Robert Guy were held in La Celle cemetery, near the Church and the Castle. Villagers came in procession, including my parents, the Riviere's and Elvire de Brissac, who as a child was living in the Castle, facing the Church. Elvire remembers very well the ceremony with the memory children have for all extraordinary events.

Almost the entire village was there, people around Elvire were saying the airmen were British. Graves have been placed in the cemetery next to the grave of Atman Raba, the French soldier killed on June 15th, 1940 when the German Army arrived. My mother who had a beautiful voice, and directed the school Choir, sang with everyone's assistance "La Marseillaise" and the "God save the King" in front of the graves covered with blue, white, and red flowers.

At about the same time, the father of Sinclair Ronald – a cousin of F/S Robert C. Guy – had landed with the Royal Scots Fusiliers, on Gold Beach near Arromanches and Le Hamel in Normandy. He was heading towards St Gabriel located 6 miles away.

Arromanches was one of the two places where an artificial harbour was built to ease all Logistics operations, Transporting equipment, Troops and help in the Repatriation of soldiers wounded.

Other funerals that day in Plaisir and Pontchartrain were for the RAF airmen of 15 Squadron Lancaster LM 575 LS-H . "Tommy" F/O. T.W. Dunk, aged 32, Rear Gunner from Bulawayo, Rhodesia and "Robbie" W/O. R.B. Aitken, aged 21, Mid Upper Gunner from Langside, Scotland. Their coffins were covered in blue, white and red flowers coming from the fields at this season and numerous villagers from the surroundings area attended the ceremonies. There was no priest for the celebration in Pontchartrain because villagers did not know what Robbie's religion was. they did not know or understand it was mentioned on the back of his dog tag. C.O.E. for "Church of England", "P" for protestant.

Germans had granted their authorisation for the burial in Plaisir, saying. "You do what you want with your Canadian, we have so many dead people in Normandy" Some Canadian identity papers had probably been found, which explains the error found on Tommy's grave in Plaisir cemetery. Some other testimonies say that the pilot had attended the ceremony. Phillip wanted to be there, but he was dissuaded to do so, for obvious security reasons.

The body of F/S George Boanson was found on June 16th, 1944 about four hundred yards from the tail of the plane along the D61 in brackens. George had been ejected like Ken when the aircraft broke apart. He also had not managed to open his parachute. He was buried next to his comrades in La Celle-les-Bordes cemetery on Saturday June 17th.

Only the dog tags on the bodies of W/O. Ken Bryan and F/S George Boanson had been found. F/S Robert C Guy was buried first as an unknown airman, clearly identified however in the Civil Register and written about by the hand of my father. he was likely to be the Rear Gunner of the plane, given the place where his remains were found in the forest near the rear turret.

My First Souvenir. June 1945

The Boy (Francois Ydier) and the Bomber (DS822) in June 1945 (author's photo).

In mid-1945, I was about two and a half years old. Following the German surrender, my father, the Town Hall secretary, was preparing to return to the RAF the dog tags of airmen buried in the cemetery. Before doing that, he went back to the wreckage of DS822 in the forest, checking around for personal items that belonged to the airmen so he could return them to their families.

My father was not aware of the RAF security rules imposed on airmen. They were not allowed to take with them any personal objects which could have helped the Gestapo to identify them and their families. In case of an inquiry, they were instructed to only give their Name, Rank and Identification number and they were all emptying their pockets before boarding the plane.

Although the tail was more than a mile from our home, my father took me with him. Probably to free up my mother who had just had my young brother Pierre three months before. He took a good quality picture with his Kodak camera probably to document the file. The child in front of the tail also gives a good scale of the remains.

The Boy and the Bomber

The picture is quite graphic – you can see the jagged wreckage of the plane. At the same time the picture also seems quite serene because of the child standing before the tail flat on the ground among trees. The picture depicts very well what happened to the plane before crashing. You can clearly see perforations from the Flak shells and machine guns made by a night fighter which probably was the cause of the death of the airmen in the rear during the attack.

To tell the truth, I had no memory of the aircraft itself. A young kid tends to only retain things at his level and I probably did not understand the sad reality that the presence of the wreck in the forest implied.

Seventeen years later, in August 1962, I found by chance the picture which was undated. I went to see my father and asked him.

- "Who is the child on the picture?"
- "It's you." he said.

My father then explained, "I went there to search for the personal belongings of the airmen so I could send them back to the RAF for the families involved along with their dog tags." I asked my father.

- "Did I have a blister on my foot?"
- "Oh yes, you gave me a hard time all the way back home, shouting like hell, it took us some time."

It was the only thing I remembered. Specifically, I remembered my mother when we arrived back at the house. She took me by one leg upside down, to take off the shoe that was hurting me so as to stop my crying. I musn't have been very heavy at that age and was for sure the only one to remember such a detail. I had as if by chance traced what was probably my oldest souvenir.

Researching Our History

In August 1962, I was a trainee Pilot in the St Yan Air France pilot school. I had there my first 47 hours of flight on a Stampe SV4, a plane like a "Tiger Moth" that was not so easy to fly. I was passing the final tests to enter the ENAC pilot school of Air France, "EPL 62". I had come back home to Vendee for the week end, right in the middle of the course.

We were flying by groups of five. The last three trainees in our group were Michel Asseline, the best one, then Jean Prunin and myself. I take this opportunity to greet them. Michel unfortunately had later a dreadful accident in Habsheim, Jean Prunin ended up his career as a Captain on board Concorde, having been the youngest Air France pilot to fly this legendary plane, trained on delta wing Mach 2.2 Mirage IV.

That course had put my mother in a rage because I had been accepted into Nantes University studying "Special Maths" which was quite a tough challenge. She was telling me that I was too clever to become a taxi driver. I could not care less, in fact I wanted to become a test pilot, as I had a passion for flying, it was a dream for me. I successfully passed all medical tests, written and oral exams and obstacles to arrive there. In addition I was paid by Air France, my first salary which contributed later to my pension.

That very day, I thought to myself, one day, I will have to write about the story of our own Lancaster, DS822. That is what I started to do, some thirty five years later.

The Quest Begins

I had often heard stories about the crash of the Bomber when I was a child. My parents never knew where the front of the plane had crashed as the Germans placed a blockade of guards around the wreck immediately prohibiting anyone from approaching. They asked themselves many questions as they couldn't understand why the three airmen in the rear did not try to bale out. The airmens' bodies had been found in the forest badly burnt, and with their parachutes unopened. Was the plane too low? Why did they not even try to open their parachutes? They did not understand.

My parents thought the nose of plane had crashed in the Limours area. They knew that the rest of the crew had baled out successfully. They never found out much more.

On 27th February 1946, the Flight Lieutenant J.J. Prior visited La Celle-les-Bordes. He met my father to confirm the name of F/S Robert C. Guy the Rear Gunner of the plane who was buried in the cemetery as an unknown airman.

F/L. J.J. Prior is probably the one who had told them what they knew about the other airmen. He also mentioned in his report that he visited Guillaume Main in Longchene, the farmer who had sheltered W/O. "Jack" A.N. Durham for about two months in 1944.

In any case, my parents could never imagine that the three airmen buried in the cemetery may have been killed during the attack of the night fighter before the crash.

The Germans forbid anybody to approach anything that had fallen from the sky. This did not help researchers to understand what had happened. It's also clear that, unlike the tail section, the nose had been cautiously guarded by the German soldiers for a while, preventing anybody to approach.

My parents were also unawares that the fourth airman who landed during the night near Moutiers had come from the same plane. The day before, the funerals of W/O. Ken Bryan and F/S R.C. Guy were held in La Celle-Les-Bordes cemetery, the providential "Antoinette" had been sent by the Comet Line to help F/S John Clarke to escape, which they surely knew. But, for obvious safety reasons, nobody was speaking on both sides, risks were too high and the Germans did not play around with the ones helping airmen.

I really started to work on the Lancaster story when I cut my professional activities in 1996. I analysed the picture of the tail. The holes in the skin clearly show the plane had been hit by Flak shells but also by the machine guns of a Night Fighter. in trying to escape to deadly beams of Flak projectors coning the plane, the pilot was forced to make sudden "corkscrew" manoeuvres at high inclines, sometimes unbearable for crews.

The first breakthrough came when I went to England to celebrate the marriage of one of my good friends' son, Serge Sireau in August 1996, another Aviation enthusiast. We were Lieutenants (F/O) together in Bretigny Sur Orge flying Test Center during our military service, from 1968 to 1970. I found by chance, when visiting an RAF museum near London, the book edited by W.R. Chorley listing, day by day, all the losses of Bomber Command during the war.

Obviously I found the bomber shot down above La Celle-les-Bordes in 1944. The book detailed her mission, the names of all the crew members and then detailed the three airmen buried in my village and the four survivors, two of which I learnt had been held as POW's by the Germans.

Two airmen were Australians (RAAF). W/O. Ken Bryan the Wireless Operator buried in La Celle and W/O. "Jack" A.N. Durham, the Navigator. Five were English (RAF) and more precisely two Scotsmen (P/O McGown, F/S R.C. Guy), one Welsh (P/O L.W.C. Lewis) and two English (F/S J. Clarke, F/S "George" J.G.S. Boanson). The names of the airmen buried in my village were familiar to me because every year, my father took his Class to pay a tribute to them in the Cemetery for the Anniversary of their deaths, on June 8th.

After the wedding of my friends' son in England, I returned soon after and visited the Memorial built in "La Petite Forêt" during the fifties in their memory and the cemetery next door. I was puzzled because the Memorial mentioned W/O. K.E. Bryan as a pilot, P/O (Pilot officer) and another passenger "Not identified" aboard the plane. RAF archives did not mention that. W/O. K.E. Bryan instead of P/O, and there was no trace of an unknown airman in the Cemetery.

A Lancaster standard crew was seven, only one pilot, sometimes eight or nine for special missions, but not in this one according to Chorley. I started searching in the surrounding counties of where the front part of plane crashed, knowing now that four airmen had been able to bale out safely.

The target for the bomber was Massy Palaiseau, east of La Celle, according to W.R. Chorley. I thought logically that the plane had been hit by Flak whilst flying over Rambouillet, causing her to go down before reaching her target. The tail picture in the forest showed clearly the aircraft had been hit by Flak and a night fighter, as I said before.

I thought she was in descent towards her target with several hundreds of gallons of fuel and several tons of bombs. The crash must have provoked an enormous explosion which, normally should have been recorded somewhere in Town Hall registries.

Following what my parents said, I was searching around Limours, following the consistent direction with the target mentioned by Chorley. I found several bombers, but not the one identified in La Celle. All my inquiries were unsuccessful, showing nothing in the surrounding counties.

The Memorial in 'Petite Foret' (author's photo).

I had few chances to find her, I did not know yet that Massy Palaiseau was not a specific target but a group of targets in a given sector. On the other hand, I did not know that the survivors had baled out on the way back from target coming from the East before the plane broke into two pieces above La Celle-les-Bordes.

I also searched for the families of the survivors in the UK, as I had their names given by Chorley. Unfortunately to no avail, a real dead end and I was about to quit, because I could not progress.

A Memorial was erected around 1950 along the D 61, a hundred yards from where W/O. Ken Bryan's body was found. Before the memorial was erected in the fifties, a simple wooden cross was placed at the edge of the road. Christiane Pochet who lived in "La Noue"a farm nearby, remembers this very well.

It was the same, for the German pilots killed in the area. a simple wooden cross painted in kaki green near the wreckage of the plane which I also remember. The bodies were then transferred to Germany in the fifties.

Deer Hunting in La Celle-les-Bordes.

In 2007, another event totally independent from the story helped me to reactivate my research. We sold the house my parents owned in Poiroux, Vendee where they retired in 1957. In emptying the house, I found by chance a small historical treasure about La Celle-les-Bordes history. Deer hunting in the late forties, written by school children (including me) under my father's supervision as a school teacher.

Every year in November a great feast was organised by the Duke de Brissac in La Celle-Les- Bordes, celebrating St. Hubert the Patron of Hunters. We were the Duke's closest neighbours in the village. My father who researched a lot of French history as a hobby knew the Brissac family. They were a very old noble family, having in their genealogy four Marshals of France and this was of great interest to him.

The last of these Marshals, who was living during the reign of Louis XIV and XV, was the brother in law of the famous diarist Saint-Simon. They hated each other, Saint-Simon was known for calling him the "Marshal of Bottles" probably due to his being a hard drinker.

For the St. Hubert celebration each year, my father would ask every child in the class to stay in different places in the county and write what was happening that day. Some drawings made by children as well as some pictures taken by my father also illustrated the document. In 1949, the former king of England, Edward VIII who abdicated in 1936, came to the ceremony with his wife, the Duchess of Windsor, a truly historic moment for the village.

In Appendix 11 is an excerpt from this document with the map of the hunt from November 4th, 1950 on which I have placed the airmen's landing points and where the tail and nose of the plane fell. There are also two pictures taken on the day of the ceremony on the 4th November 1949 with the Duke and Duchess of Windsor in the company of the Duke de Brissac.

The original document had been forwarded to the Academy Inspector at the time. I imagine my father also gave a copy to the Duke de Brissac who was deeply involved in the event and pictures. I reproduced a hard copy in colour of documents, which were drafts with original spelling mistakes. I sent it to all the editors (I was one of these) and Elvire de Brissac, all were my classmates in primary school at the time.

A special word about Elvire. she was going to school in Paris, but ended every school year two weeks before us. Her father would then send her to La Celle-les-Bordes with her governess, Mrs. Dussert. Elvire would therefore end every school year twice. I vividly remember Elvire as she had a beautiful elocution. I remember her standing on the stage in our class room reciting poems. Her governess must have had some difficulties watching her playing and sharing life with young wild children in the country, she was always one of the first to run in the woods and the fields with us.

June was also the month of the feast of St. John in the village. We would have a big bonfire and a greasy pole, under the supervision of Calixte Lernoult, a brave farmer of the village who would use buttons instead of coins for the winner's prize.

This discovery was key to reactivating my research as well as giving me an opportunity to meet my former classmates. I gained some additional testimonies and evidence for the story of "my Lanc" and I also met the newly elected Mayor, Serge Querard, who was very interested by the village's history.

Later, we met each other in La Celle, I brought the Deer Hunting dossier, and naturally in our discussion we started to talk about the Lancaster. He told me that another person, Jean Huon in Clairefontaine had also done some research and published a story about the same plane. I contacted him and went to see Jean without hesitation so we were able to put all the information we had in our hands together. Jean Huon helped open for me two paths. Ydoine Riviere and Australia.

Jean was very familiar and longstanding with the Ydoine Riviere family. The "Angel of Clairefontaine" who had buried the airmen in 1944 in the forest, a remarkable fact totally unknown to me. He had also been able through the U.K. Embassy in Paris to establish contact with Kenneth Wright in Australia.

Kenneth was another key contributor. former Mayor of Mildura, former RAF and RAAF pilot, former N°2 Operational Training Unit for fighters in WWII, former President of Senate in Victoria state, Historian in charge of RAAF museum in Mildura. I could not have dreamed of getting a better support in helping me in the research.

Mildura is a city located 360 miles North West of Melbourne, where W/O. Ken Bryan originated from. The Wireless Operator "Kenny" of "my Lancaster" has been buried in my village. Kenneth was able to establish links with the Bryan and Durham families. "Jack" A.N. Durham, the Navigator of the crew originated from Tenterfield in New South Wales.

This is how I was able to put Ydoine Riviere now living in Paris with Lisa Todd, Ken Bryan's niece, living in Melbourne in touch with each other. I also forwarded to Ken Wright for the Mildura Museum some pictures of the tail of the Lancaster in the forest, the children in the cemetery in 1946, the "Clairefontaine Angel" with Mayor Querard behind the graves.

School children in the Cemetery on June 8th 1946. The author is on the right side near R.C. Guy's grave with flowers in his right hand (author's photo).

Kenneth Wright published two articles soon after receiving these new documents in the "Mildura Weekly" a local newspaper and then later in "Wings", the RAAF National magazine, telling the Lancaster story. Kenneth also played a key role in our research, like Mayor Serge Querard, bringing his expertise and facilitating local contacts. We became very close through the internet, without knowing each other, exchanging information on a frequent basis speaking about everything and nothing.

In particular, upon Kenneth's request, I tried to complete the story with a chapter about the Underground in France during WW II and I ended up with my parents friends, the Birdsall's, involved in the "Carpet bagger" US operation and OSS. In addition, this was a side consequence from my research, a cherry on the cake, I also found "our" two Belgian Countesses Andrée de Jongh and Anne-Marie Errembault de Dudzeele…

Jean Huon had a personal relationship with the Riviere family. Mrs. Ydoine Riviere and her husband Jean Louis had lived with their parents in Clairefontaine during the war. Ydoine managed to get in touch with the Bryan family at the end of war. She wrote to them a poignant letter explaining what had happened. This is certainly the reason why the graves were not displaced (see Attachment 3) after the war, to the contrary of what was done for W.J. Buttner in 1945 and Atman Raba in 1966.

It is also, as we have seen, the reason why in Australia Kenneth Wright was calling Ydoine "The Clairefontaine Angel". On the Australian side we had the right contacts now, even though it is quite difficult to reconstruct a history of events and reconcile testimonies some sixty years later. An example among others, in reading the Australian press, P/O "Jack" A.N. Durham, the Navigator had given the bale out order of the aircraft, which should have been the responsibility of pilot. I had now three pilots in one plane which was getting too much.

I realised later, with the help of Australian archives, the reason for this misunderstanding. The "Pilot Officer" position in English is a Rank and a function. You can be a Pilot officer without being a Pilot. It was the case for W/O. Ken Bryan and W/O. Archibald "Jack" Durham. they had both been promoted retrospectively to P/O "Pilot Officer" on May 14th, their accident happened on June 8th and their promotion confirmed on July 21st, 1944.

Everything was clear now, there was just one pilot on board who gave his crew the order to abandon the plane (confirmed in MI 9 report). The inscription on the Memorial in the forest was correct (except for the unknown airman) and consistent with RAAF archives. On June 8th 1944, Ken was a W/O. in the RAF files and P/O in the RAAF files, just like Archibald.

Left to right: Francois Ydier and Ydoine Rivière with Mayor Serge Quérard October 15th, 2008 (author's photo).

In October 2008, after having met Ydoine in Paris, we visited the site in La Celle-les-Bordes where Ydoine went in 1944. We also met the Mayor Serge Querard and payed a tribute to the airmen in the cemetery.

At this stage in the research, we were missing the contacts with English families. A few months later, an unforeseen project reactivated definitely our progress, thanks, one more time to our friend Serge Querard.

Choisel 65th Anniversary

In 2009, the city of Choisel, which is not far from La Celle-les-Bordes, decided to celebrate the 65th Anniversary of the Allied landings in Normandy with the arrival of the US troops and General Leclerc 2nd Armoured division in the Chevreuse valley. The head of the council organising the Event was Roger Guernon.

Choisel is a pretty village where the actress Ingrid Bergman used to live. There is also an 18th century Castle surrounded by a beautiful park where the Marquis de Breteuil also live. This was another childhood memory, because I remembered accompanying my father when he met often with the Marquess de Breteuil to discuss his historical research on Louis XV.

Roger Guernon visited all the neighbouring communities to request information and documents on events which occured in the surrounding areas during the war in preparation for the exhibition. It was during this he met the Mayor Serge Querard who introduced Roger to Jean Huon and myself. Roger had been fortunate enough to contact the English and American families related to Servicemen who had fought in the area during 1944 and would be interested primarily in the Anniversary Celebrations. This is why we sometimes refer to Roger as Sherlock Holmes.

The Lancaster story was one of the best documented at the exhibition, and for good reasons as three English families, two Scottish and one Welsh, have all taught us so much about their relatives and what happened after the accident.

Roger had previously had some difficulties with English speaking, therefore I offered him my help. This then helped us to make a lot of fast progress. He came to see me in Plaisir, we exchanged our material and shed some light on many of the areas that had previously remained in the shadows.

Everything was further accelerated when, thanks to Roger, I got in touch with Jean and Ronald Sinclair, cousins of Robert Guy, the tail Gunner of our Lancaster who was an unknown soldier at the start due to his ID badge not being found at the time of accident. We were far from imagining what we were going to discover later.

This is yet another great coincidence in the history, as Roger had found Jean Ronald on the internet totally by chance, after finding a note sent by Jean where the name Guy was mentioned.

I also found with the help of Roger, vital records of La Celle-les-Bordes at the time written by the hand of my father, an avenue which I had not thought of before. They brought the historical truth about the circumstances of the accident on June 8th, 1944.

When I contacted the Ronald family in April 2009, we exchanged a few documents recently published, they forwarded airmen declarations to MI9, documents only given to families or next of kin. One morning Roger gave me a call. You know what, this morning a Lancaster landed in my mail box Sinclair had forwarded to us a model of the famous plane.

Soon after, Jean and Sinclair told me. "We are travelling in France in May we would like to meet Ydoine Riviere who had buried their cousin in the forest in June 1944" and true to their word, what was said was done.

The meeting was very emotional to say the least. We accompanied them on the crash site along with Mayor Querard, Ydoine Riviere, Roger Guernon, Christiane Blanluet (Pochet) and her husband Jacques. Christiane was living in La Noue farm, close to the place where the tail had fallen in the forest. When Christiane was going to school, she brought milk every morning from home, making circles with the milk pot on the way, without losing a drop of milk of course.

As we walked into the forest with the Mayor to where the tail of the plane fell in 1944, a deer crossed in front of us on the forest trail. Henri Kergreis remembered hunting in the seventies and having seen many metallic parts in the forest near the "Parc de la Verrerie". He told me one day, "We arrived in La Celle during the war without any papers. I came with my mother to school where we met your father. He just said to my mother, I don't care about papers, we'll see them later, we are not going to leave Henri at home without anything to do, bring him tomorrow morning to school".

André Billard also remembers very well having spent hours playing around the tail in the forest. It was he who confirmed he found there ½ inch ammunition in the surrounding area and thus established the presence of a ventral turret on the plane to fight night fighters attacking the aircraft from underneath, using the deadly "Schräge Musik" Luftwaffe procedure.

André is the living memory of what went on in the village, he also told me "When we had not finished our work during the week, your father made us come back on Saturday and Sunday if needed". Imagine that today? And André concluded "We did not care at all because we knew your father liked us. When we did something wrong at school, we did not say a word at home, because we were sure we would have had a second reprimand". Christiane totally agreed.

The world has definitely changed, but not necessarily for good. André was a child of the Church Choir and has witnessed first hand many of the events we are talking about in the story. Things were more simple back then, there was no counselling when a misfortune happened, you would find with the spirit of cooperation and a strong dose of good common sense the right way to settle problems.

The Ronalds brought also significant help in forwarding to us secret MI9 military archives. MI9 was the organization in charge of repatriating to England airmen shot down during combat. They were highly qualified personnel that you couldn't train within a few weeks.

This is the reason why the Gestapo gave money to those who betrayed airmen so as to keep them from returning home to England. It is to be noted that any airman succeeding in escaping was automatically transferred to another squadron for safety reasons, thus preventing any links the Gestapo may establish with names if they were shot down twice, unfortunately something which occurred from time to time.

Sinclair Ronald was another great contributor on the other side of Channel, because he had also been able to contact other English families of DS822 crew. We also started then to speak regularly in video conference. I remember one day I called Sinclair for a reason forgotten since. He said to me, "Hold on, Gillian Dean the daughter of John Clarke is here and she is going to speak to you." I spoke for the first time to Gillian and at the end of the conversation I continued to talk with Sinclair. I told him. "I don't know what the matter is with Gillian, she did not look very amicable and it looks like she swallowed her umbrella, as we say here." Sinclair then answered. "Gillian is still around, I will call you back later.

Half an hour later Sinclair called back and said. "I owe you an explanation, one year ago Gillian met a fortune teller lady who predicted she would meet a lady named Jean (Sinclair's wife and Robert Guy's cousin) who will tell her new facts about the accident her father had during the war. Gillian was very impressed when she talked to you, she thought you were a spiritual guide.

Admittedly, it was enough to ask questions, even if one does not believe in these kinds of prediction. It is thanks to the statements of John Clarke to MI9 that I discovered he had been recovered next to Moutiers and Bullion by a girl "Antoinette" and led to Chevreuse Kalmanson home, under the protection of Maurice Cherbonnier, a book seller in Chevreuse, who belonged to the same resistance network as my parents, called - "The Comet Line."

The Cherbonniers were very close friends of my parents in Chevreuse. With Dr de Palma, they contributed in the escape chain of airmen, hiding those who would help if needed and sheltering them from house to house... Maurice Cherbonnier had participated in the escape of twenty one airmen. I had never heard the name of "the Comet Line" from my parents.

Their only daughter, Janine married another RAF airman, Harry Sanderson, in 1947. They would invite him home for weekends as a host family, when he was working in "SHAPE" (Supreme Headquarters Allied Powers in Europe). The young couple had two children Anne-Marie, "Pussy" and Gerald, "Jerry". Naturally both were my companions during childhood.

John Clarke was biking in Chevreuse, accompanied by a young girl, whose name I found out through "Pussy", was Anne-Marie Errembault de Dudzeele, a Belgian Countess, the so called "Countess of Montenegro" according to my mother. She was twenty two years old and by all accounts was a very pretty woman. Her code name in the Resistance was "Antoinette", sometimes also "Marie Antoinette".

Anne-Marie was a great and unusual character. She always carried a gun with her. In fact, she was a Belgian Countess through her father, but her mother was the Princess Natalija of Montenegro. It is in memory of her that "Pussy" was called Anne-Marie. People who risk their lives together weave bonds of friendship strong and durable.

The RN 906 was blocked by German military convoys leaving for Normandy. John had taken small country roads before arriving at Chevreuse to avoid them. John hated dogs but to deceive and avoid questions from the Germans, he had carried Anne-Marie's dog Jimmy in a basket on his luggage rack. It was important that he did not speak at all, because it would have been immediately spotted by the Germans. Jimmy never failed to bark whenever he saw a German soldier, which simplified discussions and decreased the risk of being heard. From what I was told by his wife Daisy, it was then that John changed his mind about dogs.

Anne-Marie de Dudzeele walking around St Remy with Jimmy (courtesy Géraldine Cerf de Dudzeele).

Anne-Marie frequently travelled around the Chevreuse Vallée on her bicycle with Jimmy, who loved it and might well have been called "Snowy". The grandmother of Herge who designed the famous cartoons of "Tintin and Snowy" was employed by the Errembault de Dudzeele family at the beginning of last century. She had had twins in the early twentieth century and one of them was the father of Herge. The natural father of the twins was perhaps the father of Anne-Marie, who had married the Princess Natalhie Konstantinovic of Serbia in 1918, also a Princess of Montenegro through her first wedding with Prince Mirko Petrovic-Njegos… They had two daughters Helene, born in 1921 and Anne-Marie, born in 1922. This may also explain why Herge used great places of Central Europe in his stories.

Waterbeach 2009

Soon after the Ronald's visit in May another reunion of former primary school children of La Celle-les-Bordes was organised with the help of the Mayor. We first met in the former Town Hall and School, then had lunch in Cernay la Ville and later went back to the new Town Hall, where we danced to Victor Swiatly playing accordion and Johnny Boule playing saxophone.

Some of us shed a tear from enjoying finding ourselves back in our school. Serge Querard presented a collection of old post cards. The meeting was extremely moving and some attendees even recognized some of the farm horses of the time. It also gave me an opportunity to gather a few testimonies from Monique Dacheux, Johnny Boule and Henri Kergreis about the Lancaster story.

Soon after, on June 13th 2009, I was invited to attend the annual Veterans meeting of 514 Squadron in Waterbeach. I am so proud to have been able to go onto the airfield at Waterbeach, as the military base was subsequently closed in March 2013, after 72 years.

The church service was held in St. John's church in the village. During the service, the Reverend mentioned my parents for what they had done during the war to help the airmen and myself for my research on the history of flight. We then attended the "Fly Past" of a Lancaster over the 04/22 runway[9] probably the same as where DS822 had taken off from, on June 8th, 1944 for her last flight.

William McGown declared to MI9 he took off at 23.59 and Chorley mentions t/o at 00H37. This time was probably the engines starting time with a waiting time before take-off of about forty minutes which does not seem absurd for the eighteen aircraft from 514 Squadron participating in the mission that day. I checked this with Veterans at the reunion. This waiting time was enough to have engines at the right temperature and the control tower was coordinating all aircrafts arrivals on target and also with other

---

[9] The two figures painted on the ground give direction divided by ten of the axis of the track in degrees. 04 = 40° (North East) in one direction and 22 = 220° (South West) in the other direction.

planes having the task of placing coded coloured markers before their arrival on the target area. With her 5,000 lbs bomb load, I think she took the longest runway, 04/22 which was putting the plane in the right direction for France if the wind was coming from the south.

There were a total of three hundred and thirty seven aircraft that left UK that night from seventeen different airfields and an estimated total of seventy five aircraft for the Massy Palaiseau group which had sixty seven targets and eight planes to place the markers.

It was at the reunion that I met for the first time Daisy Clarke, the F/S John Clarke's wife, her children Gillian, Graham, and Rachel and grandchildren Paul and Michelle who speaks very good French. This was the day the idea came to nickname Daisy Queen of Waterbeach, "HRH" or "Waterbeach Queen" in English. I also had just learned from Kenneth Wright that the nickname for Ydoine Riviere in Australia was the "Angel of Clairefontaine" or "Clairefontaine Angel".

There was also the cousin of F/S J.G.S. Boanson, Stan Kershaw and his lovely wife Beryl with whom I had a great discussion about the number of our respective grandchildren. I was also very impressed by the strong personality of Daisy and her daughter Gillian who proudly wore the Waterbeach badge of her father on her chest against Daisy's will.

The 514 Squadron badge represents the squadron's specialism of blind-bombing through complete cloud cover.

The badge of 514 Squadron depicts a sword piercing a cloud, to symbolise bombing through complete cloud cover. This was made possible from mid-1944 when the squadron, as part of No. 3 Group, started to use GH navigation equipment. The squadron's motto *Nil Obstare Potest* translates as 'Nothing Can Stop Us',

The Mess at Waterbeach, site until 2012 of the annual 514 Squadron Reunion. The event is now held at the Waterbeach Military Heritage Museum (courtesy Sinclair Ronald)..

recognising the fact that the crew did not need to actually be able to see the target to obliterate it.

When we were waiting on the 04/22 runway for the fly past Lancaster, the condensation trail of a jet crossed a cloud in the sky, just like the sword on the badge, a true sign of destiny. This was Gillian who saw this sign first as I filmed.

There was so much excitement when the Lancaster arrived from Scotland and made several low passes over the runway making sharp turns to return around. My muscles contracted as if I was on the plane and it is with great sadness that we saw the Lancaster disappear over the horizon on its way to another Fly past. We then went to the Mess base for lunch.

It has not moved since the war, and there are still two bars. When William returned to Waterbeach with civilian clothes in September 1944, his former Rear Gunner F/S John Tanney had lent him a Sergeants' uniform and this is where William had offered him a drink in the NCOs' Bar. F/S John

Tanney and W/O. Ken Bryan's room was a few meters in the left wing of the building.

William knew then what had happened to his three companions in the tail of the aircraft. He felt responsible for the death of W/O. Ken Bryan, whom he had sent to inspect the rear of the aircraft before the attack of the night fighter.

During lunch, I was able to speak with several of the Veterans and check some assumptions I was making about actual combat operations during the war, in particular the use of the emergency exit doors when an aircraft was shot down.

Clive Hill offered to me an original lithograph of a Lancaster MKII, similar to DS822, flying over Waterbeach... I also gave copies of it to Roger Guernon for the Choisel exhibition, to my two brothers and Elvire de Brissac.

After lunch we attended the ceremony inaugurating the 514 Squadron Memorial by F. J. Noble, Commander of the Waterbeach base. We then visited the Museum which is located adjacent to the Mess.

It was a wonderful day. I felt proud to have had the privilege to share this experience with not only the Veterans but their families as it was such a great moment of dedication and forgiveness. I had spent much more time speaking to Veterans rather than with families. I was feeling guilty when I left, having not spent enough time with our friends of the Lancaster family who so kindly invited me.

We managed to catch up, as we will see later.

Choisel Historical Meeting

The Exhibit's official opening was held from during the weekend of 6th to 8th November 2009,. It had kept us busy a good part of the year. One more time, a great moment dedicated to the memory of the "boys", shot down in 1944.

We must say this occasion was unique, concentrating everybody's energy, we really had the feeling of re-making history.

Roger Guernon had spent quite some time communicating with families, gathering information about their lives and what really happened in the Chevreuse Valley in 1944 upon the arrival of Allied troops after D-Day.

The Exhibit was opened on Saturday, November 8th by Mayor C. Juvanon, in the presence of Mr Michel Leclerc De Hautecloque, the son of General Leclerc who freed Paris on August 25th 1944 at the head of the famous 2nd Armoured Division.

A plaque honouring the memory of Marcel Mithouard, who had passed away recently, was unveiled in the presence of his widow, on the same occasion. Marcel had published before a document, "An Unforgettable

From L to R. Gillian Dean, Rachel Clarke, F. Ydier, Josselyne Lejeune-Pichon, Michelle Dean, Hannah Moss and Jean Ronald. Seated: 'HRH' Daisy Clarke (courtesy of Sinclair Ronald).

Event" telling the story of the Vallée de Chevreuse Liberation in August 1944.

On this occasion, family members of the DS822 Lancaster airmen came from England, as well as Mrs. Myrna Gaignat and her daughter, from Dallas, U.S.A. Mrs. Gaignat is the sister of a Lightning P38 pilot, shot down above Choisel in August 1944. A plaque honouring the memory of Charles Gaignat was unveiled the following Thursday.

Mrs. Josselyne Lejeune–Pichon – "The Angel of 622 Squadron Mildenhall" - was attending the ceremony too. Josselyne published the history of another Lancaster MKIII, shot down the same night, LM 491 GI-E[10] as well as S/L. Phillip Lamason escape. The Kalmanson family (Denise Kalmanson, Antoine Poliet) was also celebrating the event in Choisel. They had sheltered F/S John Clarke, W/O. Ken Chapman and S/L. Phillip Lamason on June-July 1944 in their home in Chevreuse. The niece of pilot F/O. McGown, Violet Reith could not come, following a last minute impediment.

Daisy Clarke, just getting out of hospital had arrived the day before in company of her two daughters Gillian and Rachel and her Granddaughter Michelle Dean.

The cousins of F/S R.C. Guy, Jean and Sinclair Ronald were there in company of their granddaughter Hannah Moss as well as (George) F/S J.G.S. Boanson's cousins, Beryl and Stan Kershaw with their son Russell and his wife Helena.

A display of old military trucks and equipment had also been organised on this occasion. Overall, eleven family members came from England to pay their tribute and remember the airmen of DS822 Lancaster.

A dozen friends from the area in 1944 assisted greatly during the weekend and deserve our hearty thanks for their contribution to the success of celebration.

•   Serge Querard, La Celle-les-Bordes Mayor, Colonel Alain Populaire FAF, without whom nothing would have been possible, Ydoine Riviere, Clairefontaine and Paris, who buried airmen Robert C. Guy and K.E. Bryan in the forest in 1944

---

[10] "Nous Combattons De Nuit Au Squadron 622" - "Bellamus Noctu" Josselyne Lejeune-Pichon

• Johnny Boule, the first witness of the accident in 1944, who unfortunately could not come, following a health problem. He told me his regrets at not being able to be there. Johnny has sadly left us since.

• Monique Dacheux who saw the plane in flames passing above her head a few minutes before the crash, in company of her husband Henri Devilliers,

• Christiane Pochet (Blanluet) who was living in La Noue farm, close to the tail wreck in the forest, in company of her husband Jacques,

• Claudine Le Guellec (Merlino) who was living in Les-Bordes, with her husband Phillippe,

• Francis and Emilie Node Langlois, our close neighbours, who loaned their house to host some visitors, without forgetting of course Roger Guernon and myself with our spouses Evelyne and Françoise.

HRH Daisy Clarke, the Waterbeach Queen, was just recovering from surgery and was very courageous. She attended all celebrations in a wheel chair. The exhibit grand opening was followed by a cocktail in Choisel Town Hall where our English friends had the opportunity to chat with Myrna Gaignat and her daughter. These were moments of great emotion.

At the beginning of the afternoon, we all went back to La Celle-les-Bordes to attend the Official ceremony dedicated to our aviators, organised by Colonel Alain Populaire master hand, a pilot in COTAM, FAF[11].

The ceremony was held in the forest, near the Memorial dedicated to aviators which had been built around 1950 along the road, not far from the place the tail section was found in 1944. A detachment was there to present the arms, having at its head a young lady, a Lieutenant in French Air Forces. The Squadron leader, Gerry McGeary representing the United Kingdom embassy, was there too with his wife as well as many villagers, just like in 1944.

After the Service to the Dead and the national anthems, the mayor, Serge Querard gave a moving speech, translated live in English for our guests. It was raining and quite cold, which did not prevent many villagers attending.

At the end a piper, Sergeant Piper Lopez, played "Highland Cathedral" in front of the Memorial, to honour our aviators from Scotland.

---

[11] COTAM.   Commandement du Transport Aerien Militaire, FAF

Impressive moment when everybody was standing to attention. Then the old trucks of the war arrived in "La Petite Forêt".

Mrs. Solange Marchal was there too. She was living in Les-Bordes castle in 1944 and knew my parents quite well. Her brother, Captain François de Labouchere, a hero killed in 1942, had fought as a Spitfire pilot during the Battle of Britain in 1940. Mrs. Marchal came there with her family, in particular her daughter Isabelle de Lezardiere. I discovered on this occasion, that her step family owns Le Poiroux castle, the village where my parents did retire in 1957 in Vendée. Another coincidence I had not known before. More, I also discovered that the Marchal family owns also a house in Basque country, where we now meet sometimes during summer.

We laid down the traditional poppies in front of the Memorial, then paid a tribute to the aviators in the cemetery and left Poppies and flags on the graves.

Last but not least, an ecumenical service was held in La Celle church, co-celebrated by father Vilaine and Reverend Philip Mounstephen, who came from Paris for the occasion. Marie Laure de St. Exupery and Francine Auger had decorated the church with flowers as in the old times for St. Hubert and the Carnutes choir sang in English during the service. I was under high protection during the office, seated between the "Clairefontaine Angel" and the "Queen of Waterbeach."

The Mayor offered then to participants the glass of friendship, in the new Town Hall, which gave everybody some time to chat with other persons attending, a great hearty celebration overall, entirely dedicated to the boys who surely deserved it.

The day had not ended, as we then drove back to Choisel, where, just as in 1944, a great popular dancing ball had been organised in Chateau de Breteuil when US troops and the 2nd Armoured Division Leclerc arrived in the valley. Our Host, the Marquess François de Breteuil, was born a few months before, in December 1943.

Mayor Querard invited us after for a dinner in Town Hall at around 10.00 pm - thanks to time lag – to be able to establish a video conference between La Celle-les-Bordes, Saturday night and Mildura & Melbourne, Australia Sunday morning. Mayor Querard and others spoke with Mayor Glen Milne and Kenneth Wright in Mildura, Neil Bryan (Ken's brother) and Lisa Todd his daughter in Melbourne.

Ydoine Riviere the 'Clairefontaine Angel' and 'HRH' Daisy Clarke the 'Waterbeach Queen' (courtesy of Sinclair Ronald).

Pictures were displayed on a large screen in the room, an unforgettable moment. Emotion was at its peak, many shedding tears, the language barrier had been broken. We were all re-making history and celebrating the memory of airmen.

On Sunday morning, to end this historical moment, we had a brunch in my home in Plaisir in company of Mayor Querard, our British friends, Ydoine Riviere, Roger and Evelyne Guernon, organised thanks to the talent of Christiane, Monique, Claudine & Françoise and their husbands.

A Lancaster and Her Crew

The Lancaster is, without doubt, one of the most legendary planes of the Second World War. The McGowan crew were flying a Lancaster MKII. Her aircraft identification code was DS822 and her unit code was JI-T. She had been delivered to 514 Squadron at the formation of the squadron in September 1943 in Foulsham.

DS822 was equipped with four Bristol Hercules radial air-cooled engines, of 1650 HP each. It is easy to distinguish her from other types MK I and MKIII which were equipped with Rolls Royce Merlin engines that had a much thinner profile. The Hercules engines have a round shape with lateral prominent exhausts with flame arrestors easy to identify. They had been installed to prevent German night fighters being able to see the exhaust flames in the dark.

The MkII was not equipped with H2S but had instead an additional ventral turret Frazier FN 64 with two machine guns of ½ inch, installed to fight Night Fighters equipped with the deadly "Schräge Musik" dorsal guns shooting upwards[12]. André Billard, who spent some hours playing around the tail in the forest confirmed to me he found ½ inch calibre ammunition, almost twice as big as other 0.303 inch ammunition used for the three other turrets of the plane.

300 MKIIs had been produced between September 1942 and November 1943 by the Baginton factory near Coventry, with serial numbers ranging from DS 601 – 852 and LL 617 – 739. MKII production was stopped and the type phased out from operational service through 1944. The Hercules engines were then manufactured and reserved in priority for the Halifax MkIII. As it happens, the expected shortfall of Merlin engines did not materialise. Overall 7,377 Lancasters were produced during the war, a few hundred of which were produced in Canada. They were flown over the Atlantic Ocean to receive in England their final equipment. 3,249 Lancasters were shot down in combat, or about forty percent of total. The length of the Lancaster was 21 meters, her width was 31 meters and her height 6 meters.

---

[12] The existence of *Shräge Musik* was not known until the MkII had been phased out of front line service. However, it was known that bombers were vulnerable to attack from below.

The weight empty was 17 tons, with a full load 31 tons, with a bomb payload of about 6 tons or more. Later specially-modified Lancasters were able to carry the 22,000lb (ten ton) 'Grand Slam' bomb. The Lancaster's maximum speed was 240 knots or 440 km/h at an altitude of 15,000 ft., maximum range was 2,400 miles or 4,400 km with a reduced bomb load. Her maximum ceiling was 27,000 ft. or 8,200 meters.

55,573 RAF airmen died during the war in RAF Bomber Command, more than 9,000 Bombers were shot down by German defences. The number of Lancaster aircrew lost alone is over 15,000 casualties. They carried out approximately 156,000 combat operations ('ops') overall, dropping some 609,000 tons of bombs or an average of about 4 tons per mission. This was an exceptional contribution by all these heroes, who came from all over the world to defend our liberty.

The standard crew of the Lancaster was seven, sometimes eight or nine when some specific tasks were requested; training a co-pilot, radar tests, navigation systems testing and conducting airborne radio countermeasures.

Pilot. Lancasters required only one pilot but other crew members were often trained to take over in an emergency. The Skipper had the life of his crew in his hands. They would have followed him into Hell, which, in effect, was what they were doing on ops. Nobody, whatever their rank, questioned the pilot's orders.

Flight Engineer. He took care of engines, propellers, flaps, landing gear, fuel and hydraulic commands, a true flying plumber. All his tasks were tightly linked to the pilot's actions. He was acting with the pilot as in an inseparable team. He was seated next to the pilot, on his right side, at a slightly lower level.

Bomb aimer. He held the success of the mission in his hands. Along with the Navigator, the Bomb Aimere guided the pilot to the target, and decided when the bombs had to be dropped. This was after having identified the aiming point marked with coloured flares or ground markers dropped before by Mosquitoes or any other planes dedicated for this specific task. Marker colours, sequences and coordination were specified to crews during briefings.

When approaching the target, with bomb bay doors opened, the pilot could not change his direction and had to fly straight and level, to allow the bomb aimer to acquire the target. His post was in the front of the plane at the lowest level, right above the forward emergency exit and below the forward machine guns turret, which was also his post during intermediate phases of flight before approaching the target. He just had to throw out the hatch to open the forward emergency exit. As a result, the bomb aimer had the best chance of survival of all crew members[13].

Navigator. He had to get the plane on target and bring her home safely following the briefed route. This also entailed avoiding the most dangerous zones signalled during briefings, giving the pilot changes in directions due to changes in the winds at altitude and other information. Critically he had to be certain of the aircraft's position at all time, at night over blacked out or cloud-covered enemy territory. His post was behind and below the pilot and flight engineer. The navigator was seated at a small table that was curtained off, allowing him to use a small light to aid him in his calculations.

Wireless Operator / Air Gunner. He had two tasks; wireless operator and Gunner. He could replace the other gunners if they were injured, killed or needed relieving. He could also help the navigator by plotting the position of the aircraft using specialised navigation systems such as Gee or H2S radar. Because of his position in the middle of the aircraft, with the immense obstacle of the wing main spar between him and the rear exit, wireless operators had the lowest chance of survival in the whole crew, at least in 514 Squadron.

Mid Upper Gunner. He operated the central upper that Lancasters were equipped with. He had a suspended seat for the upper guns which was quite uncomfortable, especially when the pilot was making tight manoeuvres to avoid being coned or trying to escape a night fighter.

Rear Gunner. Regarded as the most dangerous post in the aircraft, for several reasons. Fighters attacking from behind were shooting at him first to neutralise the rear turret machine guns; He did not have enough room inside the turret to wear his parachute. In case of emergency he had to quit his post, put on his parachute and get out through the rear exit door or by rotating his turret and falling out backwards. The intense cold was made worse by the removal, in most cases, of a large piece of perspex to give him a clear view of approaching fighters. Gunners often suffered from the cold

---

[13] According to an analysis of 514 Squadron personnel losses.

during the long flights at 18,000 ft. above Germany with an outside temperature between minus 15°C and minus 25°C or more. The rear gunner was isolated from the rest of the crew and also spent his entire tour of ops flying backwards.

The chances of escape were reduced further because of high acceleration supported during tight manoeuvres in a combat or a spin. This may well be what happened to R.C. Guy and T.W. Dunk who were trapped in the rear turret and fell with the plane. John Tanney, Bertie's predecessor, was saying with a great sense of humour "As I was one of the shortest gunners on the base, the Germans never succeeded in killing me, their bullets were passing above my head".

It happened sometimes two members of the crew had the qualification of a pilot, the second one having the skill to replace the skipper in case of need. It happened once that a non-qualified pilot brought back the plane because the pilot had been killed during a Flak attack. In such cases there were not many solutions to save your own life. Either taking the controls or bale out if you could.

The pilot was seated on his parachute that was serving as a cushion, sitting on concrete, according to pilots. His seat was also protected by a thick armoured plate, protecting him from bullets coming from behind, the classical case of hunters shooting the bomber from behind.

The recommended procedure to bale out in good conditions were. Flight horizontal, speed 120 knots (220 km/h). Main emergency exits were. Fore part below bomb aimer post, rear part large exit door starboard side through which the crew boarded the plane.

John Tanney and Ken Bryan used the rear exit to bale out on March 31st 1944 coming back from Nuremberg at a time William was about to land almost short of petrol without seeing anything in front of him.

William had just been promoted P/O the day before, he was lucky enough to land in a field without hitting a tree or a building. No injuries among the crew left on board. John probably open his parachute too soon when he got out of the plane. His parachute was torn by the tailplane and John broke his backbone on landing with a damaged parachute. He was thereafter forbidden to fly in combat operations, which, ironically, saved his life; he was replaced by R.C. Guy. God was on his side that very day.

Building a Team

P/O William McGown was the first to join RAF in 1940 and became a pilot. He was born on October 1st 1913 in Rutherglen near Glasgow, in Lanarkshire, Scotland. He was a book seller, and was living in Great George Street, Glasgow. He was married to Margaret Catherine Lockhart but the couple could never have a family. His niece, Violet Reith remembers him very well. She describes him as a good man, quiet, a peaceful great uncle. From what I have got from his other crew members, he was older than the others and behaved like a father to them, he was about 31 in 1944 when he was shot down.

William joined the RAF on September 20th 1940, he was 27. He passed all tests, medical and others for a few months and probably started his training as a pilot early 1941. I found traces of him in George Boanson's log book, as a co-pilot for two flights in a Lancaster MKII in August 1943.

He was probably ending his final phase of training as a pilot, before being appointed Skipper. The 514 Squadron had been allocated with about 74 MKII Lancasters, or about twenty per cent of MKII Lancaster produced during the war.

In records, I found him Captain or Skipper in the fall, flying alone in Blyton, Foulsham or Waterbeach. William joined the "Commissioned services" on March 29th, 1944 when he was promoted "Pilot Officer", on March 30th, the day before his return from Nuremberg where he landed his Lancaster in England without being able to see anything in front of him and about to be low on petrol. It was a magnificent way to celebrate his promotion.

After his return to England, early September 1944 after evading capture, he was transferred to another Squadron, standard safety procedure for an aviator shot down in an enemy or occupied territory. William was promoted to Flying officer on September 30th, 1944. He then became a Mosquito pilot, a faster plane with a smaller crew, which he flew until the end of the war.

P/O Lyndon Warwick Lewis was the second one to join the RAF, on May 15th 1941, at the age of 24. He was born on December 1st, 1916, one day after Andrée de Jongh, the Belgian founder of Comet Line. Lyndon was living in Cardiff and was an active Police Officer.

He was first sent to Canada, as a trainee Pilot having probably falsified his visual tests. Having some difficulties in landing a plane properly, as one of his eyes was weak, he was reoriented to train as a Bomb Aimer/Navigator.

Upon his return from Canada, mid-summer 1943, he joined 514 Squadron at Waterbeach and he teamed with McGown from November 1943 to June 1944, having achieved 25 missions of combat before the shooting down of the aircraft in La Celle-les-Bordes. He was commissioned as Pilot Officer on March 3rd, 1944.

F/Sgt John "Jack" Clarke was the third to join the RAF. He was born in Coalville on December 11th 1922, the son of Maud and John Clarke. He was living during the war at 48, Avenue Road, Coalville. Like his father, he was working for the National Coal Board, as an employee to the Mine. He was impatient to join the RAF but he could not do it before the age of 18. He was finally accepted, soon after his 19th birthday, in December 1941.

Jack got his Engineer qualification, "Flight Engineer" on July 19th 1943 and joined 514 Squadron in Waterbeach in September. He probably started to fly then on MKII Lancasters. The brand new DS822 JI-T, was delivered just out of the factory, on Sept, 25th 1943.

The first combat operation I found with McGown is dated November 1943, for a mine laying operation in Frisian Islands in Denmark. John had probably done other training flights with his colleagues between September and November but I could not trace them in their respective log books.

W/O Jack Archibald N. Durham RAAF was born on February 3rd, 1920 in Tenterfield, Australia and was an accountant when he joined the RAAF in August 1941. He left Australia in August 1942 and arrived in the UK on November 18th, 1942. He had most probably been transferred at about the same date as John Tanney joined the RAF. Durham followed the same training courses as others in Lichfield in 1943 (27 OTU) and Blyton (1657 Conversion Unit) and joined McGown and his crew at the end of 1943.

Durham flew at least 25 combat opérations with his colleagues in France and Germany for a total of 138 flying hours between November 1943 and June 1944. I don't know if he continued to fly after his return to the UK on the 8th September 1944. He left for Australia to complete his service in Squadron 4th Advanced Flying Unit RAAF 4th October 1945, then discharged from the RAAF at 4th. AFU with the rank of Flying Officer the same day.

This implies Jack Durham made most of his combat flights with McGown. Between the end of 1942 and the end of 1943 he was undergoing training. He declared in MI9 report having three years of service with the RAF.

F/S George J.G.S. Boanson was born on June 22nd 1922, in Sunderland, North East of England. George had a priority in the Army because he was an Engineer, but he volunteered for the RAF 1944. He was called in February 1943, he was about to turn 21. The RAF needed aviators, to replace those killed in combat. George got his Air Gunner qualification in Lichfield (OTU) on May 29th 1943, after 17 training flights, 6 hours night flights and 27 hours overall.

He started to fly with McGown on August 25th 1943 in Blyton who was then a trainee co-pilot, for four flights at least. By the end of September George had thirteen training flights with McGown, including three night flights.

F/S Robert C. Guy, known as "Bertie", was also born in 1922 at Cambusland, Scotland. Bertie had a twin brother Charles M. Guy who joined the RAF like him in 1943; they were 21 years old. Bertie was a rear gunner, Charles a flight engineer. Bertie pursued training until early 1944. He had a combat mission to Berlin which aborted for technical reasons with Simmons as Skipper. He already had quite a lot of experience. 233 flight hours including 88 hours Night flights and 12 missions on Germany.

In March 1944, he flew two combat missions with Chitty as Skipper to Essen and Nuremberg, probably flying with his twin brother in the same plane, F/S Charles M. Guy, Engineer. In April he had a mission to Rouen with Topham as pilot. From then on, he carried out all his ops with William McGown.

W/O Ken E. Bryan RAAF was born on July 13th 1921, in Mildura. He had a sister Eunice born on December 1st, 1923 and a brother Neil born on February 21st, 1928. Ken first was enrolled first in the RAAF, probably in 1941. He wanted to become a pilot but he was not accepted because of his sight. He then followed a Radio Operator-Gunner training in Australia in Maryborough, Queensland. At the end of his training he was directly sent to

England, where he completed his training like others in 1943 in Lichfied and Blyton.

I found Ken for the first time in the McGown crew list on November 26th, 1943. In June 1944, he had flown 24 ops with McGown. He was about to be 23 and was promoted retrospectively in July to "Pilot Officer" on May 14th, 1944 like "Jack" A.N. Durham.

F/S John Tanney, English, was born in 1924 in Sunderland. On leaving school at the age of 14 in 1938, he became a butcher in a slaughterhouse in Ashington. When war was declared he volunteered for the RAF and his call up arrived when he was 18 in 1942. He passed the selection tests in Doncaster and then went to London, appointed to Brindlington for his initial training phase.

He went to Dalcross, now known as Inverness airport, on the Moray Firth, north of Scotland. During WW II, it was known then as Dalcross Airforce Base. He was flying in a Boulton Paul Defiant, a single engine training fighter with a post of Gunner. John wished to become a Radio operator, but having failed to pass the Morse Test, he became a Gunner. He started to fly in 1943 with a Polish Pilot with whom he had some difficulties to communicate.

514 Squadron with MkII Lancaster at Waterbeach, 1943. From right: 1st row No.3 McGown; 3rd row No. 7 to 11 Durham – Clarke - Boanson – Lewis - Tanney courtesy of Violet Reith).

At the end of May he was promoted Sergeant and confirmed as a Gunner. He went to Lichfield, "OTU" where he made several flights with several Pilots on Wellingtons. That's when the team was assembled, with three Australians, the Skipper Doug Rogers, the Navigator "Jack" Durham and the Radio operator "Kenny" Bryan.

They crashed during a training flight with McGown and an Australian skipper Ross Stanford, a well known cricket player. William McGown took the lead of the crew for the first time on July 24th, 1943. He met again his other colleagues when he went to Blyton, with George Boanson rear Gunner and John Clarke, Engineer.

He joined the 514 Squadron on October 4th at Foulsham, where the squadron had been equipped with Lancaster MkII aircraft. John Tanney said he much preferred MkIIs to Wellingtons or Halifaxes. Unlike many others, John had never been air sick during a flight in the rear turret.

From the end of November 1943, John made most of his flights with Mc Gown. He had completed twelve or thirteen combat operations by March 31st, 1944. On that day, coming back from the devastating mission to Nuremberg in another Lancaster MkII, LL683, McGown could not find Waterbeach or Stradishall, his diverting airport, because of fog.

After having circled for two hours and about to run out of petrol, McGown was forced to land without being able to see anything in front of him, thus proposed to his crew to bale out before, if they preferred to do so. The two room-mates, Ken Bryan and John Tanney decided to bale out through the rear door whilst the others chose to stay on board.

As they were flying at low altitude, John probably opened his parachute too soon which was hooked by the tailplane and was torn. The forward emergency exit was the easiest to use but obviously not without danger. The bomb doors are immediately aft of the exit and, if the doors were open, could snag the parachute. Landing in the fog and snow, John broke his back bone, which saved his life. He was taken off operations and replaced by F/S R.C. Guy, as the rear gunner post. This was destiny as the accident unwittingly saved his life. McGown also was lucky, they landed in a field without hitting anything near Sawbridgeworth, though the plane was destroyed.

Bombing Nuremberg had been a real catastrophe, with Bomber Command's highest loss rate during the war. 105 planes crashed, 537 aviators were killed, 157 were captured and only 11 managed to escape. Damage to the town was not significant. Chances of survival for the crews of the aircraft shot down that day were only one in five. Bombers had flown all the way to eastern Germany and back with German night fighters pursuing them between Belgium and Nuremberg.

March 31st had been a very bad day for 514 Squadron in particular. Six Lancaster MkIIs were lost with 20 aviators killed. Sgt. Charles M. Guy, F/S Robert C. Guy's twin brother, Engineer in LL645, A2- R crashed upon their return to Waterbeach. His plane was baulked on final approach by another aircraft, they crash landed while attempting to go round. The impact was severe and the main undercarriage unit ripped away. The skipper P/O W E Chitty RAAF was injured, two other crew members were killed. Sgt. A.B. Pattison RCAF and Sgt. J Sheperd. It is possible, but unclear, that the twin brothers were in the same plane that day, following a last minute replacement before departure of another crew member.

On recovery from his injuries, P/O Chitty RAAF formed a new crew, though retaining his Flight Engineer, F/S Charlie M. Guy. Quite often, skipper and engineer were a strong team. They were working together side by side on the plane. F/S John Tanney came back from hospital in Loughborough, Leicestershire to Waterbeach in September 1944. He was there when William McGown returned from Paris. He lent him a sergeant's uniform and William invited him to have a beer in the Sergeants' Mess.

John confirmed to him that the DS822 had most probably been shot down by a night fighter equipped with *Schräge Musik* and he thought the airmen in the rear had been killed during the attack by the night fighter. William felt guilty for the death of his wireless operator whom he had asked to go to check the rear of the aircraft when it was hit by Flak upon their return.

Thanks to the exhaustive work by Wendy Flemming about the 514 Squadron operations during the war, we have able to include the table shown in Appendix 5 page 157 *check page number* listing all DS822 crew's combat missions (and a few others mentioned in this book).

The McGown crew on joining 514 Squadron at RAF Foulsham.

From L to R 1ˢᵗ Row.   W/O. A.N. Durham RAAF, P/O W.L. McGown RAF, Sgt. J.G.S. Boanson RAF; 2ⁿᵈ Row. Sgt. J. Clarke RAF, Sgt. J. Tanney RAF, W /O.   K.E. Bryan RAAF, P/O L.W.C. Lewis RAF (courtesy of Stan Kershaw).

The Last Flight

The crews' briefing was held on the evening of June 7th, 1944. The Massy Palaiseau group comprised 75 planes, 3 Lancasters and 5 Mosquitos to mark the target and 67 aircraft to bomb it. 514 Squadron had an establishment of thirty Lancasters. Its contribution for the night was eighteen aircraft allocated to the Massy Palaiseau group. Two would have to abort the mission with compass problems.[14]

Some 127 airmen[15] were therefore at the briefing, which lasted at least one hour. During the briefing, crews were assigned their objectives and given the relevant instructions and details for the mission.

After the arrival in the room of the Station Commander and the Squadron Commander, the briefing was conducted with the display of huge aerial maps on the wall for the mission, red ribbons indicating flight paths, with the weather forecast and winds along the route, all presented in the usual thorough detail.

The Flying Control Officer gave the runway to be used for take-off and then the Intelligence Officer gave the altitude for bombing, between 5,000 and 6,500 ft that day, then the shortest route to return after the bombing. Crews were warned of danger zones to be avoided on the way.

Each of the targets would be marked by five Oboe (radar navigation system) Mosquitos who were to drop green target indicators. If visual identification was possible, the Master Bombers and backers-up would drop red target indicators. If visual identification was not possible, the orders were to bomb the centre of the green markers.

---

[14] Source. 514 Squadron Operations Record Book (The National Archives).

[15] Eighteen crews, each of seven men, plus one pilot on his initial 'second dickey' trip. That pilot was W/O Les Sutton, flying with the crew of F/L Lou Greenburgh. The Greenburgh crew was also shot down on this operation with the loss of their wireless operator. Greenburgh and Sutton evaded the Germans and were eventually rescued. Sutton returned to Waterbeach and completed a full tour. Greenburgh, on his 26th op, was transferred to Transport Command. The full story of Lou Greenburgh's exploits, *Skid Row to Buckingham Palace,* is also available from Mention the War.

The Boy and the Bomber

The Squadron Commander and Station Commander gave their final words and wished all good luck for the mission. Then all watches were synchronised. The mission required thorough coordination among a group of several hundred aviators spread over seventeen airfields.

The RAF's main objective that day was tactical attacks on German communications. Cutting all roads, bridges, railway tracks and marshalling yards would slow down the the transport of German troops and equipment to Normandy. The RAF allocated only 337 bombers on June 7th to this mission, compared with more than one thousand planes two nights before, some crews having even attacked twice the same day.

The night was clear, with cloud cover above 6,000 ft which was not good for the bombers. They would be flying further into French territory and lower than usual in order to drop their bombs accurately and minimise civilian losses. This would also give the enemy night fighters more time to intercept them than on earlier raids against targets in Normandy.

The stakes were high, the mission would have a significant impact to finish off combats against the Nazis after D-Day. There was a feeling that the Germans were about to lose the war.

P/O William McGown was by now an experienced Lancaster MkII pilot. he had already had flown 25 combat missions with the aircraft and overall he had 145 flight hours on ops. He was flying DS822 for the second time, his previous mission with the same plane and crew had been a seven hour flight to Karlsruhe and back in April (see Appendix 6). He had only aborted one mission, following an engine failure on an operation against Berlin in December 1943.

He had also been extremely efficient in coming back from Nuremberg in March when he crashed in the fog and snow without seeing where he was landing and without having anybody hurt on board. William's morale was high, he had great confidence in himself and in the plane. DS822 was equipped with a two ½ inch machine gun ventral turret to fight against German night fighters and their "*Schräge Musik*".

The task force had been split into five groups of bombers each having a specific target in each of the following areas. Acheres, Versailles, Chevreuse, Massy Palaiseau and Juvisy.

DS822's target was the railway marshalling yards in Villeneuve St Georges (VSG), a straight line distance of about 230 miles, but more like 270 as the route took into into account dangerous areas to be avoided during the flight, particularly Dieppe, Rambouillet, Limours and Versailles.

The flight plan forecast was a 3 hour and 15 minute round trip, at the altitude of 10,000 ft, with descent to about 5,500 ft for the bombing itself. This meant an average 160 knots speed. The bombs had been loaded onto the aircraft that afternoon; eighteen 500 lb medium capacity bombs for each Lancaster[16]. The fuel load was about 1450 gallons, giving a total flight time of about 6½ hours and, as a consequence, a comfortable reserve upon return of over three hours.

P/O W McGown knew the mission would be risky, but certainly less than his earlier ops over Germany. The crew had had time to rest since the bombing of Ouistreham in another MkII to prepare the landing grounds for D-Day. The airmen had a short time to rest after briefing and get mentally prepared for the fight. By now, for McGown and his crew, it could almost have been considered routine.

W/O Jack Durham and P/O Lyndon Lewis had noted instructions carefully to bring the plane on target safely and accurately and colours utilised to mark their target. They would be flying below the cloud cover which was at about 6,000 ft. From miscellaneous information gathered in archives, we have built up the following realistic flight plan probably close to what actually happened that fateful night.

After the briefing, the airmen had emptied their pockets of personal belongings, were handed their escape kits, parachute and a "Mae West" as long as they were flying above the channel. At around 23.00 pm, one hour before the scheduled take off, the crew boarded the plane on Tarmac through the right aft exit door.

Once at their respective posts, the crewmen started to prepare the tasks they would have to perform during the flight. The skipper P/O McGown began the check list, helped by flight engineer F/S John Clarke and other crew members. William recalled he started engines at 23H59. Following his check list, having all four engines running, soon afterwards he taxied his plane to join the queue for take-off.

---

[16] 514 Squadron ORB

The Boy and the Bomber

FLIGHT PLAN   DS822 JI -T   JUNE 7-8, 1944

Bomb Load	18 x 500 lb = 4.0 tons[17]
Target	Marshalling yards Villeneuve St. Georges (VSG)
Colour Markers Green (centre of greens) or Red	
Fuel carried	1250 gallons
Flight Hours	3H 15 min Round trip
Safety reserve	3H 15 min
To VSG flight time	1H 40 min
Return to Waterbeach	1H 35 min

PLAN ACTUAL

Start Engines	23H30	23H59
Take off	00H00	00H37
June 8 Arrival on Target	01H40	02H17

FLIGHT
Time elapsed

Arrival Channel (Hastings)	+ 00H30	alt. 10,000 ft	01H07
Arrival France (Dieppe)	+ 00H20	01H27	
Arrival Dreux – begin descent	+ 00H30	01H57	
Descent to 5,000 ft	+ 00H10	02H07	
Arrival on Target VSG	+ 00H10	alt. 5,500 ft	02H17
Return Waterbeach	+ 01H35	03H52	
Fuel upon return	750 gallons (3 H 15mn flight)		
Plane missing (MIA)	+03H15	June 8th 1944	07H07

---

[17] The 514 Squadron ORB records that all aircraft on this operation carried 18 x 500lb bombs, which would be the maximum number of such bombs. Aircraft invariably carried the maximum possible bomb load which, given the risks entailed in conducting bombing operations, made perfect sense.

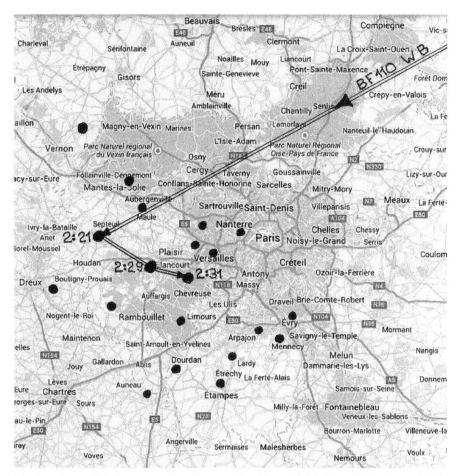

The locations of 20 Lancasters shot down on the night of 7/8th June 1944, along with the flight path of Borcher's Bf110 night fighter (IGN map).

The control caravan gave the clearance for take-off at 0H37, June 8th on 04/22 runway, the longest at Waterbeach, heading 220° south-west. It was always a short moment of stress for the pilot and the engineer, trying to get the full power from the engines, raising the tail at 90 kts, take-off at 120 kts. It took less than thirty minutes to climb to their 10,000 ft cruising altitude. DS822 flew over Hastings, heading nearly due south at 170 ° and started crossing the English Channel at around 01H07 am.

87

Major Walter Borchers flew the Messerschmitt Bf110 night fighter. The ungainly aerial array made the aircraft a formidable predator in this role (courtesy of 514 Squadron Society).

Twenty minutes later they arrived near Dieppe and started the flight over France. Keeping the same course, he went towards Dreux where he arrived half an hour later. It was around 01H57.

Starting the descent, William turned left from south 170° to east 90° and headed towards the target, VSG, at their 5,000 ft bombing altitude.

The route passed over Rambouillet, Versailles and Limours; they were however supposed to avoid danger zones protected by Flak. The approach to VSG went well, the navigator had the confirmation from the wireless operator that the markers had been placed on target. With bomb doors opened, Lyndon just had to perform the last calculations and judge the right moment to drop bombs, which he did at around 2.17 am; 9,000 pounds dropped on VSG marshalling yards.

William made a sharp turn and started immediately to climb, heading towards Massy Palaiseau and Limours in order to escape as soon as possible from the searchlights, weaving between their beams. They were caught in a beam and coned; the searchlights would not let the Lancaster escape, once she had been caught in their clutches.

One of the port engines and the tail were hit by explosive shells from the flak. Holes in the tail port vertical fin confirm the shells were at a high angle as if the aircraft was in a sharp turn, the same shell made a large hole in the vertical fin and the tailplane.

Right after this first attack, confirmed by the crew to MI9 in their eventual debrief, William asked wireless operator Ken Bryan to go and check the condition of the rear of the tail which had been hit by flak. Ken was the

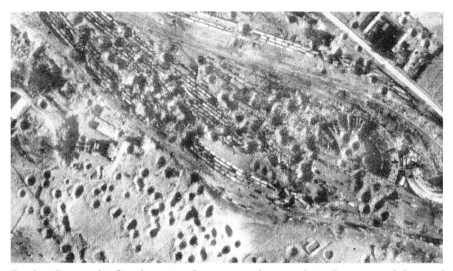

Bomber Command inflicted massive damage to railway yards in Germany and Occupied Europe. The photo above shows the effect of a visit to Giessen in December 1944 (Crown copyright).

only one whom William could ask, without risking the safety of the plane, and this was absolutely routine in such circumstances. Any other skipper would have done the same thing.

At that moment Major Walter Borchers patrolling at an even 4,000 ft altitude, arrived. DS822 was flying at 6,000 ft, the Lancaster was easy prey in the night. Walter had already shot down two Lancasters a few minutes before, one above Tacoignieres at 02H21 am and one above Plaisir at 02H29 am. It was then 2H31 am according to Walter Borchers' log book.

Borchers' Bf110 had certainly hit the engines and the rear part of the plane up to the tail, killing or injuring the three airmen in the rear as his shots penetrated the fuselage. The fusillade of fire extended to two engines, one on each side and inside the fuselage.

The plane was lost. As she was now approaching Bonnelles, William gave the order to abandon the aircraft. Her altitude was 6,000ft, flying horizontally, speed around 120 kts. She had changed her direction to the north west, perhaps in an attempt to escape the night fighter.

The outbound route from Waterbeach to Massy Palaiseau (above) and the route taken by DS822 when leaving the target area..

Lyndon opened and threw out the forward escape hatch, which was right under his post; Archibald, John and Lyndon baled out in that order.

William was left alone on board, uncertain as to the fate of the three airmen in the rear, he switched on the autopilot and jumped out in his turn, having just passed over Monique Dacheux's house. The Germans shot at him during his parachute descent at around 450ft, probably soldiers stationed in Les-Bordes castle, who like Monique had seen the plane in flames passing above. He landed on Les-Bordes plateau, near the road heading to Auffargis.

The plane, left alone with two engines running, turned to port, going into a spin. After two or three turns, the plane broke into two parts under the G-force, right before the rear exit door, which may have been opened before by the airmen in the rear preparing to bale out.

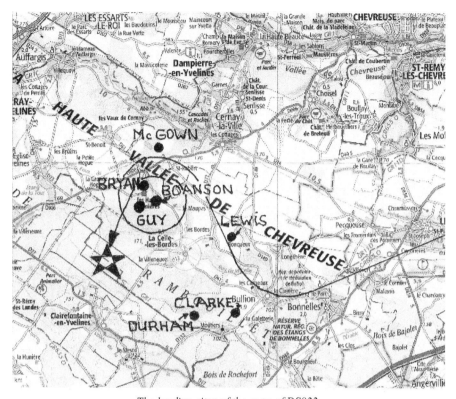

The landing sites of the crew of DS822.

W/O. Ken E. Bryan and F/S George J.G.S. Boanson had been ejected from the fuselage when the plane broke up (it is almost impossible to climb out of an aircraft in a tight spin) but they did not manage to open their chutes.

They had been badly burnt inside the plane and most probably killed during the attack of the German fighter, as well as F/Sgt. R. C. Guy who was trapped in the rear turret. My parents never knew where the nose of plane fell, they were speaking of Limours as a possible place where the nose crashed. They never linked the tail with the nose of the plane, it was another county. The wreck of the nose was most probably guarded by Germans, which did not help investigations. With one hundred foot wings, four engines weighing more than one ton each and five hundred gallons of gasoline left on board, there was certainly a huge explosion when the nose of the plane

91

crashed, debris flying within half a mile radius circle, and fire spreading in the forest around.

The explosion was certainly heard in La Celle-les-Bordes, but it was just another explosion during the night, difficult to know where it came from. As there were no other victims than three airmen, apart from a few rabbits, pheasants and deer, no records were produced other than those from forest guards in the area. Unfortunately, we were not able to trace Waters & Forests archives.

Evasion

Pop Seddon's Halifax III had been shot down by German fighters before arriving on target. His entire crew baled out safely and landed around Rambouillet. All survived and were protected by the local Resistance. They all managed to escape and celebrated the Paris Liberation in the area. The highest in rank, the Canadian Navigator F/O. Bill Leishmann, told their story in "Behind Enemy Lines". We do not think his book has ever been published, we found only an English draft in personal papers belonging to Anne-Marie de Dudzeele.

His account of events identifies without any ambiguity Anne-Marie that he probably met after the end of WWII. It brings an interesting live testimony of what happened in the Paris area from June to the end of August 1944.

The four aviators left in the front part of DS822 had baled out in the following order through the forward emergency exit of the plane.

(1) W/O. Jack A.N. Durham	Navigator,	
(2) F/Sgt. John Clarke	Engineer,	+30 seconds
(3) P/O Lyndon W.C. Lewis	Bomb Aimer,	+30 seconds
(4) P/O William L. McGown	Skipper.	+60 seconds

Let's follow this order of arrival of airmen on the ground with the statements given to MI9 upon their return to England. They describe accurately their escape route after they landed in France.

The advice given to aviators in Spring 1944 was to remain hidden in the area if they could, waiting for the arrival of Allied forces, instead of trying to escape back to England.

This is what Jack and William did and they were back at the end of August or early September 1944. John and Lyndon were betrayed along their escape route and were held prisoners by the Germans. They were only freed after the German surrender in May 1945.

The Boy and the Bomber

W/O Jack A.N. Durham, RAAF

"I baled out first from the plane, through the forward escape hatch and I landed two miles to the West of Bonnelles, between two trees which explains why I had a few bruises. It was about 2.30 am. I hid my parachute, Mae West and harness in the bushes and began walking in the direction of the North East up to 8.00 am. I sat down to take some rest and soon after, I saw four Frenchmen arriving.

They all began talking to me at once, I did not understand what they were saying, but I was able to get accross to them that I belonged to the Royal Air Force. They advised me to remain where I was until 10.00 am. At about 10.00 am, two other men arrived with some food. At the end of my meal, they took me to a farm house nearby where someone had an English dictionary.

They asked me what I wanted to do, I said I wanted to know if they could shelter me. They answered they could not do it because it was too risky for them. However they pointed out for me a road to follow taking me to Cherbourg. At the conclusion of our discussion, they drove me back to another hiding place in the bushes, recommending me not to start before midnight.

A short time after, being still cautiously hidden in the bush, another man arrived. He drove me to his home and gave me a bed and food. The next morning, Friday June 9th, I was given a message in English asking if I could stay here one month or so. I answered "yes" remaining there in Longchene, until a US cavalry unit arrived in Bonnelles on August 15th.

Unfortunately, US soldiers merely passed straight through the town, with the result that afterwards the Germans returned killing a few Frenchmen.

On August 18th, the US Army came back. My friend, Monsieur Guillaume Main, went to see them, telling them I was in his house. Finally, on August 23rd, when I was patrolling around with F.F.I.[18] we met a reconnaissance unit of the 7th Armoured US Division. I was immediately taken under the protection of US Army."

---

[18] FFI, Forces Françaises de l'Intérieur, French Resistance Libération Movement

Paris was liberated a few days later on August 25th by General LeClerc and the 2nd Armoured Division.

Guillaume Main, the farmer who had hidden Archibald, passed away a few years ago. We have spent some time with the transcription of names written in English. we have the choice between Monsieur Guillaume Main as mentioned in F/L. J. J. Prior report who met him in February 1946 or Monsieur Marcel Guillaumain? Both have existed, and we have not been able to confirm which the correct one is. We apologise in advance for families of a possible error in the transcription of the correct name.

We could not get other testimonies about the time Archibald spent in Longchene area. Somebody told us he had a strong personality and some controversial discussions with his host when he was in his home. We do not know how faithfull such a statement is. It is fair to say hidden airmen were like lions in a cage as Mrs. Cherbonnier used to say, not having the right to speak, and their hosts had quite some trouble preventing them from being identified outside and betrayed.

According to Australian Archives, Jack A.N. Durham came back to England at the end of August a few days before William Mc Gown. His interview with MI9 is dated August 26th, 1944.

F/Sgt. John Clarke

F/Sgt John Clarke baled out second, right after Archibald. "After the attack of a night fighter on the return journey, the aircraft caught fire, we had the order to bale out and I landed in a field, near the village Moutiers (close to Bullion and Clairefontaine) 40 km south-west of Paris.. During my descent by parachute, which lasted about five minutes, I saw my Lancaster in flames crashing in the forest nearby.

After having hidden my equipment, according to procedure, I hid myself up in a wood nearby until daybreak. I spoke to a villager passing through with a horse cart. He took me with him to a house located about one mile away and invited me to go in. I was reluctant to enter because I was unsure of the Frenchman, but three other Frenchmen arrived, they recognised my uniform and they took me inside.

The owner of the house gave me civilian clothes and put me up for the night. The next morning, thus Friday, June 9th, a French girl came to see me. She said she was in the Resistance movement, and after having checked my identity, she said I would be leaving the house the next day.

On Saturday, June 10th, I followed the owner of the house on a bicycle to another place one mile away, where the girl met us. We know now it was Anne-Marie, "Antoinette". The meeting point was in Bullion sector according to archives (François Prompsaud – Comet Line) which mentions in a note dated September 29th the evacuation of an airman in Bullion area, it is most probably John.

Anne Marie had a fox–terrier barking whenever he saw a German soldier. She installed her dog, "Jimmy" in a basket on John's bicycle luggage carrier, a convenient way to minimise conversations with occupants. This story had been told to me for the first time by HRH Daisy Clarke. At this time John did not like dogs very much; he has changed his mind since.

With that story in mind, we have been able to get a confirmation from other archives and a picture of Jimmy in a basket, on Anne-Marie's bicycle. To avoid their identification by the Germans, all airmen were declared deaf-and-dumb.

"Anne-Marie told me we should go to Chevreuse, we took first side roads, passing through Choisel and ended the trip on the main road (D 906) going to Paris, filled with German convoys rushing up to Normandy.

As we entered the village, Anne-Marie showed me on the left, a green painted shop which was Mr. and Mrs. Cherbonnier's library. She told me I could go there in case of emergency, they are friends, and we arrived in another house, around mid-day in the village, most probably the Kalmanson's house as we will see later."

We must say now a few words about Anne-Marie, code name "Antoinette" in "Comet Line", an exceptional Belgian lady who helped the airmen shot down in the area to escape throughout the war. Her true name was Anne-Marie Errembault de Dudzeele. She was living with her parents and her sister Hélène in "Moulin des Clayes" in St. Remy-les-Chevreuse.

It is clear now that the "Montenegro Countess" my mother was speaking of with great consideration can only be Anne-Marie. She was a Belgian Countess, through her father, the Count Errembault de Dudzeele, diplomat. Her mother, a widow who married the Count in 1918 was by birth a Princess of Serbia and a Princess of Montenegro from her first wedding with the Prince Mirko Petrovic Njegos. Anne-Marie must have had a great coolness and strong guts to do what she was doing with German officers living in her home, a few yards from her.

John arrived a few minutes later to a large house, a few hundred yards from Moulin des Clayes where Anne-Marie was living. He probably stayed there a few days[19]. It was the home of Gabriel and Germaine Kalmanson, they had two daughters Colette, Denise, and one son, Daniel.

John surely thought he had landed in paradise after having been through Hell, when the Kalmanson's took him into their home, under the protection of three beauties of the Chevreuse valley. Their grandfather had not been informed either of the presence of an airman in the house, and the Kalmanson family was also facing an extreme risk in sheltering airmen because of their Jewish roots.

The funny thing is John had spoken later to his wife Daisy about Anne-Marie's dog "Jimmy" but never said anything about the beautiful ladies who were helping him to escape.

Colette Kalmanson (on the right) and her friend Josette Albert in 1944 (courtesy of Antoine Poliet).

---

[19] See Appendix 4

In Appendix 4, a document produced by the local Liberation Committee testifies to the passage of aviators sheltered in their home during the war. The transcription of names from English to French is not accurate as usual, but the document leaves no room for error and clearly identifies them. Ken Chapman and Phillip Lamason (see pictures) and most certainly John Clarke who becomes "Ioher Clark" instead of "John Clarke".

The Kalmanson house was ideally located because you could walk from it to the St. Remy railway station, the terminus of the track to Paris. John was probably transferred a few days later to Paris in company of Anne-Marie. It should be noted that John had to walk about two miles between two stations on the way. The Sceaux line track had been cut by the June 8th bombings as Phillip Lamason says.

It was in the same house that Squadron Leader Phillip Lamason, from New Zealand, pilot of a Lancaster MkIII who took off from Mildenhall at 00H42, arrived on July 9th after having spent a few days in the Cherbonnier's book store with his Navigator Ken Chapman who was fluent

Colette Kalmanson, Phillip Lamason and Ken Chapman (courtesy of Antoine Poliet).

Squadron Leader Phillip Lamason RNZAF, DFC and bar (Crown copyright).

in French. His Lanc had been shot down the same night above Plaisir, he was also part of the Massy Palaiseau group. He had been sheltered first with his navigator Ken Chapman at Mr Cuillerier's home in Montfort L'Amaury.

Anne-Marie visited them there in the company of F. Prompsaud from Rambouillet. Phillips speaks in his memories of a "Belgian girl", Francis Cuillerier, who was about twelve at the time, remembers very well airmen hidden at his home. Anne-Marie said to them, if everything works fine, you will be back in the UK in two or three weeks.

For obvious safety reasons, underground networks were carefully split. Each member knew only a limited number of persons participating in the transfers from house to house. When a transfer included several branches, the one bringing a group of airmen never spoke to the one taking the relay with the group.

Airmen could not speak, they would have been immediately identified. They were all declared deaf and dumb. A Historian making some research on the Underground during the war, found amazing the Gestapo did not ask questions about the number of deaf and dumb which appeared during the war in the Paris area.

Maurice Cherbonnier and the Doctor de Palma were close friends of my parents, living in Chevreuse, they also contributed during the war to airmen escapes. Doctor Dugue and the pharmacist, Mr Grish also sheltered airmen, according to Anne-Marie Sanderson. The pharmacy in Chevreuse could very well have been one of the places where John could have been brought to in Chevreuse.

Maurice Cherbonnier has clearly been identified as a member of the Comet Line network. My parents never mentioned the name in front of me, even though they were dealing with the same people. According to my mother, they knew perfectly well the escape track through Portugal (Lisbon) and Spain (Gibraltar), up to 1943. Airmen on their side were observing strict safety rules. They were supposed to only declare their name, the Rank and Matricule number engraved on their dog tag (ID badge).

John Clarke was arrested in Paris by the Germans about one month later, betrayed by a traitor, Jacques Desoubrie, who was French, though the illegitimate son of a Belgian father.

Desoubrie had established a profitable business with the Gestapo and contributed to the arrests of hundreds of aviators and Resistance members. As a double agent, he had infiltrated six Resistance networks and probably got from the Gestapo several hundred thousand euros.

It is to be noted that other members of Phillip's crew, were also helped by Comet Line, Mrs. Germaine Meys living in "Les Mousseaux" Pontchartrain. F/L. J. Marpole RAF, Engineer, F/O. L.H.J. George DFC RAF, Wireless operator and F/O. G.A. Musgrove RCAF Bomb Aimer. They were successful in their escape, going through the Comet Line/MI9 Freteval camp, Desoubrie had not, hopefully, infiltrated the entire network. Mrs. Meys became later an honorary RAF member, her grave in Pontchartrain has a RAFES plaque, the "Royal Air Force Escaping Society".

John's arrest occurred in Paris on July 19th following an identity check in the street, a trap organised by the Gestapo with Desoubrie's help. John declares that he would have avoided arrest if he had turned right instead of left, at the street corner. However he would have probably just postponed his arrest by a few days.On July 23rd, Phil Lamason and Ken Chapman were taken to Paris by Maurice and his 18 year old daughter Janine, who purchased the train tickets in St. Remy railways station. They were arrested soon after, like John in Paris. Janine and her father were "skating on thin ice".

One week later, on July 30th, during a bombing operation on German defences in Caen, Lancaster MkII LL733, JI-S from 514 Squadron was lost without a trace, most in the English Channel. It will be recalled that her skipper F/L. W.E. Chitty, RAAF and flight engineer Sgt C.M. Guy had been involved in a serious crash on March 31st upon their return from Nuremberg.

Charlie Guy had not survived for much longer than his twin brother Robert "Bertie" Guy, an unbearable loss for their family, Charlie's name is commemorated on the Runnymede Memorial, see Appendix 9. We know now that LL733 most probably collided with another Lancaster I HK 558 (skipper F/S C.G. Nairne, RNZAF) in the clouds at around 08.00 am on their way back or forth to their targets located near Caen. According to our research, a body was found and identified in the channel by an English minesweeper HMS "Hannaray" It was HK 558 skipper, F/S C.G. Nairne (RNZAF); he was buried at sea the same day, following the seamen's tradition.

John Clarke, Phil Lamason and Ken Chapman were jailed in Fresnes until mid August 1944. In research carried out by Josselyne Pichon - "Jo" for her RAF friends - about the deportation of her father in Buchenwald, she found that in August he was put on the same horrible train as our airmen. Jo discovered a message left in a book by John Clarke when he was jailed in Fresnes. *"In France June 7 1944, captured July 19, always there (Fresnes) August 1st 1944"*.

Jo found this sentence in English in the book *"Wild Justice"* which helped prisoners to communicate inside the Fresnes prison. As mentioned before, Jo also wrote the story of another Lancaster MkIII, LM491 GI-E of 622 Squadron which was also part of Massy Palaiseau group. The plane was probably shot down on her way to target by Walter Borchers that night and crashed in Tacoignieres. The entire crew was killed and buried in Tacoignieres. Jo's father was in the Underground and had also been arrested by the Gestapo, jailed and tortured in Fresnes, before being sent to Buchenwald like many others. Jo lost his trace when he was there and she has never been able to find the date and the circumstances of his death.

Phil, Ken and John were transfered to Buchenwald on August 15th, just a few days before Marcel Dassault who had refused to work for the Germans in 1940 and had been jailed thereafter.

Under the terms of the Geneva Convention, airmen should normally have been imprisoned in special Prisoner of War (POW) camps, usually in Germany or further east. They should never had been transferred to camps such as Buchenwald, where they were treated like criminals. However the Germans maintained that they were not prisoners of war because they had been arrested with civilian clothes.

The 'Little Camp' at Buchenwald was an isolation unit annexed to the main camp. Conditions for the prisoners in this unit were worse even than those for the main camp population. The 168 airmen held at Buchenwald were held in the 'Little Camp', not knowing that the Germans intended to execute them (Crown copyright).

The conditions of their transfer to Buchenwald were horrible; they were treated like cattle, their journey lasted five days in freight wagons and they endured long walks when the tracks had been cut by bombing. It is to be noted that ten days later, Aug 25th, Paris was liberated by General LeClerc and many prisoners released from jail at about the same time. Somebody gave a realistic reason to explain why Germans were rushing prisoners to concentration camps. They wanted to have as many prisoners as possible in Germany to be able to use them in an exchange.

Their detention conditions in the camp were horrible too, with food which was only a light soup with small pieces of bread and worms. Phillip had established friendly relations with a French doctor from Poland, Alfred Balachowsky, who had also been deported to Buchenwald but was conducting medical research in the camp. This is why Alfred managed to give some meat from time to time to Phillip coming from animals he was conducting his research with.

On their side, the Germans were trying to break the morale of prisoners, asking them to do debilitating tasks like pointlessly moving stones from one place to another. Thirty five thousand prisoners died in this camp, as a consequence of the bad treatments they were supporting. As Phillip said, for most people, once they arrived in Buchenwald, the only way to escape was as "smoke through the chimneys".

Phillip decided with his comrades they would not join the dead. He installed discipline among the group of airmen, an example which was making their guards very mad. He started to discuss with camp management about the conditions of their detention, which were incompatible with the Geneva Convention.

One day Phillip was about to be shot inside the camp, with twenty guns aimed at him. The officer present did not give the order to shoot him though nobody knows why. Prisoners were hanged, not shot, when sentenced to death, according to Jo. Seeing that all his requests had been rejected, Phillip managed to establish contact with the Luftwaffe and the Resistance, sending the message that German airmen would receive the same treatment when they were prisoners of war.

An order had been issued in the camp saying that all airmen would be executed on October 25th, 1944. Phillip had seen the written instruction in German but did not say a word to his fellows. A few days before being executed, all aviators were transferred to Stalag Luft III at Sagen, a camp reserved for airmen, on October 19th, 1944.

Phillip Lamasons' intervention had saved the life of 168 airmen (82 Americans, 48 English, 26 Canadians, nine Australians, two New Zealanders and one Jamaican) who were transferred to Sagen camp, on October 19th, 1944. This is the camp where the real-life "Great Escape" had taken place the previous March a few months before. It is to be remembered that most of the aviators who managed to escape were recaptured and executed by the Gestapo instead of being returned to the camp.

This story was only revealed 39 years later by Phillip during an international conference held in Canada about their detention in Germany. This gives us an opportunity to pay tribute to Phillip Lamason for what he did during the war and the exceptional role he played when he was a prisoner. Some of us have suggested he should deserve to have his name given to an airport somewhere in the world, as it has been done for other great aviators.

Phillip Lamason DFC knew King George VI of England and his daughter, HRH Princess Elizabeth, personally. One day the King had asked him to "buzz" Buckingham Palace with his plane, which he did in a Lancaster with a few other fellows following him without knowing where they were heading.

I received the visit recently of Ngaire Nystrup, born in Dannevirke in New Zealand. She lives in Denmark but she has known Phillip Lamason personally for about fifty years. Her brother Hoani worked on Phillip's farm in Rua Roa for a few years, coincidentally. Ngaire saw Phillip a few months before he passed away. That day, Phillip wanted her to stay in his home to continue to speak about what he did during the war. She declined the invitation because she had several hundred kilometres to drive to end her journey, which she regrets now.

John Clarke remained in Sagan camp – Stalag Luft III – until January 1945, then he was transferred to another camp – Tarmstedt – from February to April 1945. He was freed by the 2nd British Army on May 2nd 1945, in Lubeck.

John returned to England and answered MI9's questions about his escape and conditions about his detention in Germany on September 8th 1945. John left the RAF the year after.

P/O Lyndon Lewis

"I jumped third in the row, right before our skipper William McGown. I stopped counting at 5 instead of 10 before opening my chute, being afraid of opening it too late in the dark. I landed near les-Bordes, in a field between two woods. I buried my equipment and my parachute according to procedure to avoid the discovery of my landing point and I started to walk in the direction of Paris for about 6 miles. I then hid in a wood, until day break.

At around 12.00, on June 8th, I arrived at a farm where I was recognised as an RAF airman. The farmer sheltered me for one day and a half, he gave me civilian clothes, without which I would have been immediately arrested.

Following the route to Paris, on Sunday June 10th, I stopped in another farm. I was strongly advised not to go to Paris, as it was full of

Germans, but to go in the direction of Caen, in the opposite direction. I then arrived in Chateau La Fontaine where I met a teacher who drove me in the direction of Dreux.

On June 11th, I took the road to Paris-Epernon and arrived on June 12th in Chateauneuf. I was taken in for one night by a family and on June 13th, arrived in Brezolles. A young German stopped me to see my identity papers, I knocked him out, hid him in the bracken and went on my way."

Knocking out the soldier is probably putting it mildly. Airmen were trained in unarmed combat and knew how to kill with their hands in a few seconds without making any noise. Anne-Marie probably killed a German in similar circumstances with her revolver, this is probably what she said to Bill Leishmann on June 10th in Poigny La Foret, who in return wrote, I will never forget how "efficient" she was.

"On June 17th, passing through Moulin-la-Marche, I arrived in La Halte-du-Rendez Vous, (Orne). Local Resistance integrated me in their group. I was lodged, fed and clothed and I participated in sabotage and terrorist actions.

On July 23rd I went to a farm with another Resistance Group located two miles South of Vimoutiers for one night, then to another farm, 8 miles to the West. After that I joined the Montreuil Underground group where I stayed for the rest of my "free" time.

I once went to the North of Falaise, trying to cross the front line between Allied forces and the German Army, but we failed. I never had any problem in doing what we were doing, except I was fighting with an active Communist Resistance group.

On August 16th 1944, with Canadians bombing Trun village about 2 miles away, we were ready to move at day break, having established the right contacts and arrangements having been made. The Germans, who were installed a few hundred yards from us, then circled the farm where we were and captured us. The guide organizing our movements, myself and Major Nathan Feld, USAAF, Sergeant Pergandez, Sergeant Peter Reeve and Sergeant Hutchinson, all from Canada and RCAF. I have solid reasons to think we had been betrayed by the Mayor of Montreuil. A few days before, he met two of us in Montreuil with another farmer and a farm hand working for him. He had immediately fired his worker, threatening to declare him as a Resistance Member to the Germans.

Our guide who was held prisoner together with us, advised us several times before, the Mayor had declared if a British aviator wanted to escape or get sheltered, he had to be informed. The entire village knew where we were hidden in the farm and said nothing. Upon the Germans request, the Mayor had built trenches and defences lines around their camp. The Germans who arrested us had circled us for two days and thought we were Frenchmen coming from the Caen area to avoid the fighting.

They arrived all around us, with automatic weapons, and prepared to fight. The Feldwebel leading the attack shouted. "Hands up." I obeyed and he said in a perfect English. "That's what I was told, they are English airmen".

We were first jailed in Bernay prison. On August 20th we started walking in the direction of Rouen. We were attacked by a USAAF plane when we were at about 15 miles from Rouen. Major Feld was badly hurt during the attack. Having not received any proper care from Germans, he died the next morning at around 8.30 am. Sergeant Pergandez and myself were also wounded. The two other Sergeants and our guide took advantage of the confusion during the attack and escaped.

I was then held prisoner, in bed and hospital, most of the time in the following camps.

ROUEN Hospital	.	21-23	August
AMIENS Hospital		23-28	August
LIMBURG Stalag XII A		03-17	September
OBERUSEL Dulag luft		18-26	September
BARTH Stalag Luft I		4th October 1944 - 5 April 1945	

I was freed from this last camp by the Russian Army, on May 1st, 1945."

P/O William Lachlan McGown
The pilot's statement to MI9 was recorded at Waterbeach on September 7th, 1944, the day after his return to UK. It had taken just three months for William to come back[20].

---

[20] (Ref. I.S 9/W.E.A.-8-158-876)

The Boy and the Bomber

"I took off from Waterbeach (Cambs) on June 7th at 23H59 in a Lancaster MkII for a bombing mission to Villeneuve St. George's marshalling yards. On leaving target on the way back, plane was shot up by Flak, wing port side and an engine starboard side set on fire.

I gave the bale out order and landed myself at around 03H00. Someone fired at me when I was at about 250 ft. I landed safely in a wood near Auffargis. I buried my parachute and equipment and started walking East towards Paris.

At around 13.30 pm I spoke to a man working in a field, near a farm. He gave me civilian clothes and some food. I continued walking in the outskirts of Paris and spent the night in a wood. Three days later, continuing walking, a woman contacted a Resistance group and I was taken to St. Sulpice De Favieres, where I stayed about ten days.

The Germans having found some RAF men were in the village, I joined a Maquis group with RAF Sergeant Dodds and Sergeant Ecclestone. Several days later the three of us left by train to Chelles where we did stay for about three weeks.

On August 7th we were staying in a farm near Trilbardou. 18 days later, we came back to the Maquis for about one week, before being installed in the village of Fresnes Sur Marne.

On September 1st, the Americans entered the district and I left on my own for Paris, leaving the two RAF Sergeants in Chelles. I then contacted the American Allied Commission and subsequently left by air for the UK on September 6th, 1944".

The story continues with John Tanney's testimony, the predecessor of R.C. Guy, who was just back from hospital and welcomed his skipper in Waterbeach.

John lent a uniform to William, still with civilian clothes. William invited John to have a beer in the Sergeant Mess. William was unaware when he arrived back at Waterbeach of what had happened to the three airmen in the rear of plane. He felt guilty for the death of Ken Bryan whom he had asked to check the conditions of the tail, after the Flak attack.

According to procedures, an airman shot down was automatically transferred into another squadron to avoid the Gestapo establishing links in the RAF organization, if the aviator was once again shot down. As a

107

consequence, William ended up his career flying with the RAF in 162 Squadron as a Mosquito pilot (like Walter Gibb), a faster plane with a crew of two, pilot and navigator. He could very well have had the opportunity to shoot down Walter Borchers, which in fact Walter Gibb did.

Escape of the crew of Halifax III LK 863 NP-C

In "Behind Enemy Lines", Bill Leishman describes in details the crew's escape, after their meeting with Anne-Marie on June 9th. They celebrated all together in Paris the "Liberation", after four years of fighting, and witnessed the end of "Occupation" in the Paris area. Their testimony is of great interest.

We left the café - "Au petit Paris" - soon after German soldiers. We almost suffocated with exhaust gas of the truck which took us to the main road in Rambouillet, in a house mentioned by F. Prompsaud in his report.

The next day we went in another place, along a road close to a military German camp that we could watch from inside the house. We had strict orders not to stand behind the windows, show no light and don't speak loudly.

Then we moved into a farm (a Cider house?) until early July near a chateau. We couldn't locate the place with indications given. We witnessed several dog fights above our heads with bullets whistling around, and German convoys heading to Normandy.

We cycled to Paris to a flat located on the second floor of a building down town, near Notre Dame. We could there change our clothes and shoes, then we moved in a suburb, Fontenay aux Roses, taking the Metro and a Suburban train.

The Resistance chain was very well organised, we did not have to speak, and each Resistant leading us never spoke to the next one on meeting points, in the chain.

We spent two weeks in a pharmacy, trying to read the local paper, listening to the BBC (after news in French), and trying to follow progress of allied troops. We had found a road map between Cherbourg and Paris and we were plotting on the map the location of allied troops every day.

We were given stolen tickets to get rationed food, we had bread and some food with them. We then moved to a farm, in the near suburb, handled by a couple of Britons very different from Parisians. They were just simple people, with a golden heart, constantly complaining about the Germans. Many people were going back and forth in their farm, queuing – German soldiers included - every morning to get milk, an ideal place to be unseen. Food was excellent, the best that we had had since our arrival in France.

General LeClerc arrived at about the same time and liberated Paris on August 25th. The US troops had stopped to let him get in first. We witnessed some violent actions in the street. The last combats between Germans and Resistants, the groups of FFI gathering women who had "collaborated" with the Germans and judging them in the street with a 'popular tribunal'. They were beaten, their hair shaved publicly. To protect them, the police intervened and put them in jail.

A policeman who had helped us, introduced us proudly to his Captain in the police station. I will never forget the sad spectacle of cells underground, full of shaved women with torn clothes, following the bad treatments they had been given in the streets.

For about three days, there were great celebrations everywhere following the arrival of General LeClerc. We, along with those who had hosted us, were congratulated publicly in Fontenay-aux-Roses Town Hall. The Mayor made an eloquent speech, in front of a large crowd gathered for the occasion. When we left, the Resistance lined up and fired shots in the air.

After four years of frustration, popular joy was everywhere, which was quite easy to understand, everybody was happy to get rid of the stress. The Germans left in a great disorder.

A great dancing party had also been organised in the chateau de Choisel to celebrate the event. The young Marquess Henri François de Breteuil was born on December 5th, 1943.

The Germans quit in August the Chevreuse valley in great confusion. Elvire de Brissac has an amusing memory about the departure of the Germans from La Celle. Having requisitioned the Château for their needs, on the night of their departure the soldiers stole all the clothes belonging to her nanny, Mme Dussert. So for a few days, the nanny having no clothes left, Mme Courson lent her a few clothes of her own.

Elvire's nanny was a thin young woman whilst Mme Courson was a quite fat old lady. So for a few days everybody was laughing in the village at Mme Dussert, floating literally in her clothes, until she got new ones.

The Underground in France during WW II

We have seen, through the airmen's statements, how the Resistance was working on the ground to help aviators shot down by the Germans. In our story, the chances of escaping for those who survived being shot down were about one in two, this certainly being the average of 514 Squadron. 35 evaded, 34 were held prisoners of war. To put these figures in context, however, 429 of the squadron's airmen were killed in combat or accidents.

On the ground, there was a wide variety of situations and outcomes. The risks for helpers were very high. They were really playing with their lives, facing betrayal and denunciation. The Gestapo gave 10,000 francs (about 2,000 euros) or more to those helping them to denounce helpers and catch airmen trying to escape. The airmen themselves were also quite vulnerable with the language barrier, hiding in a foreign country.

At this stage, it is useful to give a general overview of the Resistance in France, who largely contributed to the victory of Allied armies after D-Day, in particular in giving accurate location of German troops and artillery. Casualties in Resistance have been estimated to about 100,000, a figure which sounds credible, even though reliable statistics do not exist.

In May 1940, German troops invaded Western Europe. On June 17th Marshal Petain stopped the fighting which had already killed 100,000 soldiers in 37 days and announced on the Radio he had taken the lead of the French Government and asked the enemy to cease fighting.

This announcement made my mother crazy. She had endured, as a teenager, WW I and its horrible consequences on French territory. She used to say, "I lost my pride that day".

My father, who had also been on the battlefield during WW I, was trying to calm her. For him, Marshal Petain was still WW I greatest hero. He was saying Petain saved the life of hundreds of thousands of men, which as a fact is quite true.

My parents were never able to reach agreement on this sensitive issue. For me, as a child, I had two versions of the same story at home, I learnt at a young age, that judging events that you have witnessed, is not simple and requires some thorough investigations.

The same day, General de Gaulle fled to London. He obtained from Churchill, whom he met in the afternoon, the authorization to make a speech on the BBC calling for the continued resistance.

His wife Yvonne and their three children were then in Carantec, Britany, in a house about thirty yards from my friend Lartigau's house. This was another coincidence in our story. I bought a house in Basque country, thanks to Jean Claude Lartigau and I can view from my terrace the place where Andrée de Jongh was arrested in 1943.

It was decided with Churchill's agreement, to despatch a Supermarine Walrus seaplane to take Mme de Gaulle and her three chidren to Britany. The seaplane belonged to 10 Squadron, RAAF. She left Mount Batten base near Plymouth at 03.00 am, for an unknown destination in "North Britany". Her mission was secret, nobody did know – except the crew – where the sea-plane was going.

The Walrus crashed near Ploudaniel after having been shot down by either the German or French army, we will probably never know which. The four men in the crew were killed in the accident, two Australians and two Englishmen, who were buried in Ploudaniel cemetery. They were pilot F/L. John N. Bell, RAAF 24, F/S Charles W. Harris RAAF 31, Captain Norman E Hope, Intelligence Service, speaking French and Bernard F Novell, Engineer RAF, 25.

The same day, Sunday June 18th General de Gaulle made his famous BBC historical speech calling for the pursuit of combat.

His wife was totally unaware that a plane had been sent to try to bring her back to England. She left Carantec in a car heading in the direction of Brest. It broke down on the way but was successful in reaching Brest with her three children before the departure of the last ferry to England and the arrival of the Germans. God was obviously on her side; because of the car breaking down she arrived in Brest one day later than planned. The ferry she was supposed to take the day before was sunk by the Germans with no survivors.

General de Gaulle's call on June 18th marked the beginning of Resistance and the creation of Free French Forces, FFL - Forces Françaises Libres – symbolised by the Lorraine Cross.

Two million prisoners had been sent to Germany, 80,000 of them had managed to escape during the summer and had joined clandestinely.

The Boy and the Bomber

SOE, the Special Operations Executive, had been created in July 1940 by Winston Churchill to support the operations of miscellaneous Resistance Movements in occupied zones. SOE was acting independently from the War Office and the Intelligence Service. Sections F and RF were acting mainly in France and were independent from FFL.

SOE had about 13,000 members, of which about a quarter, 3,200, were women. A great friend of Anne-Marie de Dudzeele, Lise Baissac from Mauritius, had in September 1942 been one of the first women to be parachuted by the SOE over French Territory, in the Orleans area with Andrée Borrel. Lise was about 37.

In 1942 the Resistance carried out, on average, one attempted attack per day against the Germans. These attempts brought heavy punishment with executions or deportation which was not a better treatment. Andrée Borrel was captured by the Gestapo in June 1943 and jailed in Fresnes as were many others. In July 1944 she was taken to Struthof-Natzweiler camp in German-occupied Alsace where she was executed by lethal injection upon arrival, her body being incinerated. She was 24. A memorial in Valencay pays a tribute to the 104 SOE section F agents executed by Germans during the war.

The Service du Travail Obligatoire (STO) – Compulsory Work Service – in Germany, was imposed by the Vichy government from 1942 to 1944 mainly for young adults from 20 to 22. Some riots started in March 1942, young rebels, "réfractaires", refusing the STO instead joined Clandestinity or Maquis. Unfortunately, the Maquis was still an Army without weapons.

A demand to deliver weapons had been made to London in 1943. It was first refused, considering it was premature to organise rebellion in France, before the landing of allied troops. Jean Moulin, a former Prefect had been sent by General de Gaulle to organise the Resistance in France and unite miscellaneous movements which had been spontaneously created on the ground in 1940. Jean Moulin was arrested by the Gestapo in June 1943 and died under torture on July 7th, 1943 without having revealed anything. By then the number of daily attempts in France had been multiplied by ten, to about one per hour.

A clandestine press had also developped as well in the entire country, with newspapers like Combat, Libération, The number of "Maquisards" was about 25,000 but they were still without weapons, RAF Bomber Command concentrating all their efforts in the massive bombing of Germany, as explained before. The parachuting of weapons really started on December 1943.

For the first time in November the Maquis got out of the dark and organised a défilé in Oyonnax, bringing flowers to the WW I Memorial singing "La Marseillaise". Everybody was waiting for D-Day and the landing of Allied troops, but nobody knew where and when it would come. On the German side, construction of the Atlantic wall had started under Rommel's supervision.

From January to June 1944, 50,000 people had been deported to Germany. In March 400 Maquisards had been killed in Vercors. Churchill had finally given the green light to parachute weapons on French territory. Soon after Carpetbagger operation was started, organised in the UK by the USA and OSS from the Harrington airfield in Northamptonshire. With the help of OSS, establishing communications on the ground, 1,700 successful parachuting operations were organised above France and the Netherlands with B24 and Westland Lysanders between January and September 1944.

U.S. Colonel Paul Birdsall was in London at that time. I have been able to establish he was a member of OSS, so he was for sure involved in "Carpetbagger" support operations. In a second phase, droppings continued on North West Europe, in Denmark and Norway in particular.

At about the same time, several cities in France started to get rid of German occupancy. Orleans, Lyon, Rouen and Rennes. Systematic sabotages were organised to destroy different domains of infrastructures. Each plan had a given colour code to designate a same group of objectives. Railroad tracks, Bridges, Water supply, Electricity, Telephone.

On June 8th, 1944 – our fateful day – 617 Squadron successfully dropped a 'Tallboy' bomb on the Saumur railway tunnel crossing the Loire river, stopping railways being used to the South West of France for the rest of the war. They were the famous "Dambusters" who had breached two of the Ruhr dams in 1943.

Limousin was the first province to be freed. As a retaliation measure, Nazi Barbary started to react violently. The entire population (642) of a small village, Oradour Sur Glane (Haute Vienne) was exterminated on June 10th,

1944 by an SS[21] division passing through the village and rushing to the Normandy front[22]. Our friends, the same day, had been buried in La Celle-les-Bordes.

In mid-July 1944 the Republic had been reinstated in most large French cities. The FFI, Forces Françaises de l'Intérieur, were organising Resistance on the ground, with the Croix de Lorraine they were the symbols of France getting rid of German occupation.

On August 1st General LeClerc landed in St. Martin de Varville in Normandy with the 2nd Armoured Division "2nd DB" which had been assembled in Morocco during the winter 1943-1944. 4,200 vehicles including 200 tanks, 16,000 men and women, including 3,600 arrived from the former Colonial Empire and foreign volunteers and the famous Medical Divisions of "Rochambelles" and "Marinettes". They actively contained German troops in the Falaise and Alencon areas around August 17th.

Their mission thereafter was two-fold.

(1)   To progress in the direction of Paris,
(2)   To allow the return of General de Gaulle and re-install the Republic.

General LeClerc met General de Gaulle in Rambouillet on August 22nd and presented his action plan for liberating Paris. Active FFI and Resistance contributions significantly helped the fast "2nd DB" progress, signalling all points where German forces were installed. On August 6th, the panels here below had been displayed everywhere asking the population to help FFI, to participate in combats and attacks and neutralise the enemy whenever it was possible.

After having neutralised the German resistance in Trappes, Saclay and Palaiseau areas, General LeClerc entered Paris on August 24th where street fights had started on August 16th. He rapidly took control of the situation and freed Paris on August 25th, after having obtained the surrender

---

[21] SS – Schutzstaffel. Formed originally to provide security for the Nazi party, the Waffen (armed) SS was a significant military force in WW2, and was implicated in much brutality and numerous war crimes.

[22] The massacre was carried out by the *Der Führer* Regiment of the SS Panzer Division *Das Reich.*

of General Von Choltitz in Police Headquarters, who had not followed Hitler's instructions to destroy the city before surrendering.

A leaflet announcing the call to arms by General de Gaulle on 6th April 1944 (courtesy of Roger Guernon).

World War II in La Celle-Les-Bordes

Let's see now how life was organised during the war in La Celle-les-Bordes.

The Germans arrived in La Celle-les-Bordes on Saturday, June 15th, 1940. My mother had left the day before, without knowing how to drive a car with my sister, 6, and brother, 2, and the teacher replacing my father, who was on the battlefield.

Her journey was quite an adventure, I asked my mother many times to write the story, but she never did. It took her one day to drive to Vendée where my parents had a house near Les Sables d'Olonne. Her car, once arrived there, stopped and never started again for a few months.

My mother learned how to back a car when a soldier explained to her how to do it, after she had blocked a military convoy on the road.

Before, she had been out of gas in the forest near Ablis taking small roads. When she was there, thinking about what she could do with two young kids in the forest, a Spanish man arrived on a bicycle. He asked my mother, what are you doing here, and she explained. The man said, give me money, I will bring you back gasoline.

My mother thought 'I have nothing to lose', and she gave him money. One hour later, the man came back with gasoline and my mother asked him. Why did you do that? His answer was 'French people saved my life in 1936 when I was fleeing from Spain. Since that time, I help everybody that I meet having a problem.' God was on her side.

One hour later, arriving near Orleans after having crossed the Loire River, she was forced to park and go in an underground shelter. After half an hour she decided to leave the shelter. The night was clear she could drive without using the lights (which were forbidden) and she left.

One hour later, the shelter was bombed and all the people inside died. God was certainly with her once again.

She arrived in Vendée in 24 hours, the mayor of our village made the same trip in one week, arriving too late after the bridges had been destroyed by bombings. God had been on her side all the way through.

On June 14th, the Germans bombed La Villeneuve without doing any damage. On June 15th, the soldier Atman Raba, was killed with his motorbike when the Germans arrived. He was buried in La Celle cemetery with a crescent instead of a cross on his grave.

Overall, troops crossing the village did not bring any serious problems. The army requisitioned les-Bordes castle from July 13rd to 15th August 1944, and La Celle castle from August 15th to September 10th. My friend André remembers very well the passage of German troops in the village. The Château was used as a meeting point for convoys heading for Normandy.

The SS Panzer Division *Das Reich*, passing through in July 1944, behaved shockingly, as related above. Otherwise, relations with Kreis Kommandantur installed in Rambouillet were cold but correct. Some requisitions were imposed to the county, but were not carried out in totality. Many dog fights occurred above the village without bringing any serious threat to the population. The only large bomber which crashed during the war in this area, was DS822 which fell in Petite Foret on June 8th.

Several Resistance groups were created in the area in 1940, like "Vengeance" in Dourdan or Comet Line later which undoubtedly, was the most efficient organization to repatriate airmen shot down in the north of France or Belgium, and has been credited with more than eight hundred escapes, an exceptional result.

Apart from difficulties from a human standpoint to achieve such evasions, the time required to train an operational airman was between one and two years and expenses associated around 50,000 euros. It is easy to understand why Gestapo were developing so many efforts to catch airmen shot down in occupied territories.

MI9 department in London had been created for that purpose, to help the repatriation of airmen in the best possible conditions. Their archives were only opened to families recently, this is the reason why we had a difficult time documenting the history of DS822 before we could speak to families.

Lyndon Lewis's case was the most difficult. At the end of war, he continued his military career in the Security Service MI 5 and his records totally disappeared from the archives. The same applies to Genevieve Proix, probably for the same reasons.

During the spring of 1944, with Allied armies landing imminent, recommendations made to airmen were to stay hidden if they could in the place where they landed, instead of returning to England. This is what

McGown and A.N. Durham did, they were back three months later in England and avoided being jailed.

We cannot speak about evasions of aviators without mentioning now Comet Line and its Belgian founder, Andrée de Jongh. My mother was often speaking of this chain of evasions for airmen without mentioning the name, passing through Basque country and Spain or Portugal. Andrée de Jongh was a Belgian girl, 24 years old when she created the organization helping Belgian soldiers to escape 1941, with her own money at the beginning. Her code name was "Dedee" or "Petit Cyclone" or "Small Cyclone" in English, name that her father had given to her. She was carrying everything with her.

Andrée was the older daughter of Frédéric de Jongh, born in 1897, a primary school teacher in Schaerbeck, in the North of Brussels. A Graduate from a School of Decorative Arts, she first joined the Red Cross in May 1940. Very quickly she integrated a small Resistance group conspiring against the occupant.

The description my mother gave of a so called "Countess of Montenegro" was fitting her profile quite well, a confusion that I made when I began research, that I understood later.

Two Belgian Countesses

Andree De Jongh

Andrée carried out her first evasion mission in 1941 in the Basque Country, paying with her own money. The attempt involved one English airman and two Belgian soldiers. The mission failed because the escapers were arrested in Spain and deported soon after they had crossed the border. Andrée then realised that to succeed, it was essential to have a contact in Spain to help evaders and pursue their escape to England.

With that purpose in mind, she met the British consul in Bilbao and tried to convince him to help her, which was far from being easy in the beginning. Many people in British organizations were reluctant to help unknown people who could very well be infiltrated German agents.

Then the consul put her in touch with Michael Creswell, situated in Madrid, who was the local MI9 representative, whose mission was to repatriate airmen shot down in occupied territories. After the cooperation of MI9 was obtained, Andrée received directly financial help from Britain to organize escapes.

Once they had crossed the border and reached a safer area, Andrée was "delivering" airmen to Michael Creswell and was coming back to France with the Basque smuggler Florentino Goicoechea, a smuggler who was paid also to help them in a mission which was no doubt a risky one. Money was not the main concern of Florentino.

"Dedee" the leader of "Comet Line" was 26 in January 1943 when she was arrested by the Gestapo in Urrugne during her 23rd transfer of aviators. She had been betrayed by a Spanish valet, Donato, who was working in Thomas Enea farm nearby. Andrée had used his services before, during previous escapes.

She was using farms close to the mountains and the Spanish border as their last relay in France. The evasion group comprised Florentino the smuggler, Andrée and escaping airmen. They crossed the border during the night, using smugglers tracks, six or seven hours walking in the dark. Once arrived in Spain, they would cross the Bidassoa River when weather conditions were good and waters not too high.

It was not an easy task, walking in single file in the dark, without being able to see anything in front of them. The Germans patrolling the river banks frequently. During one of these crossings, one American airman and one member of the Resistance, Antoine Durcelles alias "Jacques Cartier", drowned in the river.

Florentino was leading the group, he was the only one who knew the track, and from time to time was taking a bottle of alcohol, hidden along the river. Andrée was

War heroine Andree de Jongh pictured after the war (514 Squadron Society).

the last in the file, completing the group. One day, an airman exhausted by the walk, said he got back the courage and the force to go on, just watching her walking. On another occasion, Florentino had crossed the river Bidassoa with an airman on his back.

They were arriving after in a less dangerous zone, where the risk of being arrested by the Spanish or German police was much lower. A MI9 representative was taking them with him, sometimes in a diplomatic car. Airmen passed through Madrid first, then Gibraltar, taking a plane or a ship to go back to England.

At this point, Andrée would leave the convoy with Florentino and went back to France. They were using several farms in Urrugne before crossing the border to avoid people who may notice their passage.

During their last voyage, they had spent the night at a farm, "Bidegain Berri", owned by Frantzia Usandisaga, a young (34 year old) widow with three children and a valet, Juan Manuel Larburu. They had spent the night in the farm because weather conditions were too bad to cross the river.

The Boy and the Bomber

The valet Donato who betrayed Andrée, Frantzia, Juan and three airmen would have got 10,000 euros from the Gestapo, five times the price paid in the Paris area. He fled to his native village of Cestona in Spain, where he stayed hidden for a while. In 1965, he married a woman from Vidiana and passed away on January 23rd 1983.

'Passeur' (smuggler) Florentino Goicoetxea (courtesy Riding the Comet).

Florentino, the "passeur" that the Germans actively sought, avoided capture and probably death, when he saw unusual movements of German soldiers around. He did not show up for the rendezvous.

I have found a witness to their arrest in 1943. Mrs. Elisabeth Mendiburu, who was 17 at that time, living in Urrugne. She saw the prisoners, hands on their heads with armed German soldiers behind, taking the bus in Urrugne going to Bayonne. In the film "Le Dernier Passage" the conditions of their arrest in Franzia's farm are pictured accurately. F/S Stanley Hope, one of the airmen arrested with the group testifies to this. They were not shot when the Germans seeing their dog tags, realised they were RAF airmen.

Two other coincidences; Elisabeth is the step mother of Perrine, a lady helping Françoise from time to time when the grand children are here. More, from the terrace of my house, to the right of Urrugne church, I can see the place where the arrest occured in 1943.

They were first jailed in Bayonne, for about twelve days. They were transferred to Bordeaux for another twelve days and then back to Bayonne for three months, where they were put together with the Dassie family, who

121

had been arrested after inquiries on March 11th, 1943. They were all then transferred to Fresnes, the prison where John Clarke would arrive one year later.

The three English airmen, F/Sergeants William Greaves, George Ross and Stanley Hope, were separated from the group and sent to camps reserved for aviators. F/S Stanley Hope who had been shot down on December 8th, 1942, was transferred to Stalag Luft 1. F/S William Greaves and F/S George Ross were transferred first to Fresnes, then to Stalag Luft I-IV-VI in August 1943.

Andrée was tortured in Fresnes. She revealed that she was at the head of Comet Line, but the SS did not believe her. Instead of shooting her – the standard sentence – she was deported to Ravensbruck Camp with her accomplice Frantzia, Marthe and Lucienne Dassie, who was only 15 at the time. Geneviève Anthonioz de Gaulle and Virginia D'Albert Lake, an American lady belonging to Comet Line as well, had also been transferred there at about the same time.

Juan Manuel Larburu was transferred first to Compiegne, and Buchenwald on January 19th, 1944. The he was sent to Dora camp, where V2 were manufactured. Being a Spanish citizen, he was hoping he would be freed rapidly, but he died on April 4th 1944, He was 32.

Jean Dassie was also transferred to Compiegne then Buchenwald on January 19th, 1944, he was 50. He was freed in May 1945, but did not survive long, due to bad treatment he had in Buchenwald. He passed away in Paris hospital La Salpetrière on May 29th, 1945, tragically, only one day after seeing again his wife and daughter.

Frantzia Usandisaga was very devoted, she was very anxious to have left behind her three children Mayle, Thérèse and Jean. She died in Ravensbrück on April 12th 1945 at the age of 36, following the bad treatment she received from Kapo[23]. Andrée de Jongh was freed by Allied Armies in April 1945 at about the same time as Geneviève de Gaulle and Virginia D'Albert Lake.

---

[23] Kapo, etymology unclear: Prisoners acting as guards or supervisors of work details. They were appointed by SS in camps, receiving extra rations.

Juan Manuel Larburu (left)fled to France from Hernani in 1936 (during the Spanish Civil War). He was a valet in the farm "Bidegain Berri", working for Frantzia. Deported to Germany (Buchenwald) like other men, he disappeared from the archives in March, 1944 (courtesy of Ion Zabaleta).

Florentino Goicoetxa (right) soon after his evasion from Bayonne hospital. Confined to bed, he was hidden in Charles Gaumont apartment in Biarritz (courtesy of Antoine Lopez).

According to Virginia's memoirs[24] it is unlikely that she met Andrée when they were in Ravensbrück. Marthe and Lucienne Dassie were freed soon after. Marthe passed away in Bayonne on September 7th, 1947.
A Basque memorial stone sculpture near the War Memorial in Urrugne commemorates the memory of Frantzia Usandisaga and Juan Manuel Larburu.

Frederic de Jongh, who was in Bayonne the day before his daughter was arrested, took the leadership of Comet Line after his daughter and went to reside in Paris. Unfortunately, he was also betrayed by Desoubrie in 1943 and shot in Mont Valérien with another member of Comet Line on March 28th, 1944, he was 47.

Memorial to Juan Manuel and other interned or deported patriots (author's photo).

---

[24] "Autobiography of an American woman in France" Virginia D'Albert Lake

Florentino was arrested on June 26th, 1944 by a German patrol who surprised him and shot at him on the French side of the border. He was hospitalised in Bayonne. His evasion was organised on July 27th 1944, one month later by Comet Line and he remained hidden in Biarritz until the Armistice.

Marthe and Lucienne Dassie were decorated by the French Army (Military Medal) on July 14th, 1947 in Bayonne. Florentino was awarded the Légion d'Honneur on June 2nd 1977 in Biarritz. He passed away in July 1990, his grave is in Ciboure cemetery facing the sea. A plaque honouring his memory from RAFES (Royal Air Force Escaping Society) and Comet is displayed on his grave.

A minor detail, Andrée was born one day before Lyndon Lewis on November 30th, 1916 and died a few months after Lyndon in October 2007. Andree received decorations from many nations at the end of war including the USA, England, France and of course, the King of Belgium, who gave her the Rank of Lieutenant Colonel and made her a Belgian Countess in 1986. An exceptional lady whose memory must be honoured, Andrée devoted her entire life to others in humanitarian actions. She never got married; after the war she went to Africa to take care of lepers in Congo, Cameroon, Ethiopia and Senegal.

Anne-Marie Errembault de Dudzeele

My mother had participated on several occasions in the transfer of airmen to Paris or St. Remy Les Chevreuse. She was always speaking of an exceptional girl she had met on several occasions, among other persons. It was not easy to impress my mother. She had left by car La Celle-les-Bordes in 1940 without knowing how to drive a car with the Germans on her back. My father had strongly recommended her to leave the village before, he was well informed of the fast advance of German troops, but she refused to abandon her post.

My mother, when she was speaking about airmen's escapes between 1941 and 1943, always ended her story speaking about this woman, whom she referred to as the "Countess of Montenegro", who came once to our home. She knew quite well the route followed by train from Paris to Bayonne or St. Jean de Luz, crossing the Spanish border in the Basque Country, then on to Portugal or Gibraltar.

In fact, thanks to our research with Anne-Marie Sanderson and Josselyne Lejeune Pichon, we have been able to trace her without any doubt. Her name was Anne-Marie, her code name in Comet Line archives was "Antoinette", sometimes "Marie Antoinette".

She was actually a Belgian, Countess Anne-Marie Errembault de Dudzeele, living in St. Remy-lès-Chevreuse with her parents and her sister Hélène in the "Moulin Des Clayes", an old Watermill which had been requisitioned by the Germans in 1941. She was 20 in 1942, her parents were totally unaware of what she was doing in the Underground, with a few German officers at home. What she was doing required tremendous bravery.

It was her mother Nathalie, who was in fact a Princess of Montenegro, by her first wedding with Prince Mirko Petrovitc Njegos. Anne-Marie was a Belgian Countess through her father, the Count Gaston Errembault de Dudzeele.   The American Sculptor Edward Bruce Douglas was the owner of the Watermill, he married a french woman Marthe Legret, from Britanny. They had met in 1927 on a ship crossing the Atlantic Ocean to Europe, another story of 'love at first sight'.

At the beginning of the war, the Douglases went back to the USA. The Watermill was rented or looked after by Anne-Marie's parents, the Count and Countess Gaston Errembault de Dudzeele, an ancient Belgian noble family whose roots have been traced up to the Middle Ages. The Douglases had probably met the de Dudzeeles before the war, the Chevreuse valley had in these times, many artists living around, singers, musicians, and actors.

The house, shaped like an L, was adjacent to the waterwheel. During the 12th Century it was producing flour, then it was converted to the processing of skins for tanneries installed in the valley, and production of electricity at the beginning of 20th century. The Watermill is located between two branches of the Yvette River, on a five acre land, with a two meter high cascade and a dike – now fully automated – which regulates the flow of the Yvette River.

Anne-Marie had a strong incentive to keep secret and hidden her activities in the Underground. The Douglas family history would merit a

Moulin Des Clayes/Watermill, St.Remy-lès-Chevreuse (courtesy of Nicolas Ruelle).

book in itself. Edward's grandfather was the rich founder of the Quaker Oats company.

His roots were in Scotland and he died in 1912, on board the Titanic, refusing to board lifeboats before children and women.

From 1941 to 1944 German officers occupied the first floor of the base of the L, adjacent to Edward Sculptor workshop. According to Suzanne Siffroi, the daughter of Douglas and Dudzeele's cook, the German officers were using the rooms in the first floor for guests, about 15 yards away from de Dudzeele family apartments. The apartments de Dudzeele family occupied are located on the right side.

It is now clearly established that the "Countess of Montenegro" my mother was refering to, could only be Anne-Marie. A Belgian Countess through her father, whose mother had been a Princess of Montenegro. You cannot invent such details.

Anne-Marie was travelling with a bicycle and her fox-terrier Jimmy, she always had a gun with her. She was fluent in English, which certainly gave her a central role every time new airmen were arriving. Nobody in the Moulin knew her role in the Comet Line, which was confirmed to us by her daughter Geraldine, Suzanne Siffroi and Roger Boschet. Roger's father had a Wine store in St. Remy, Roger was delivering spirits to customers. He was surprised by Anne-Marie alcohol needs. In Appendix 8 she confirms in a poignant letter sent to Mr and Mrs. Baillon, the pork butcher delivering meat to airmen, that her code name was Antoinette.

F/O Canadian Bill Leishmann Navigator in Pop Seddon's Halifax met her only once, in Poigny-la-Foret. He writes Anne-Marie had killed a German. This is not something that you invent and, in a way, is not so surprising. If one day, a German had surprised her in company of airmen, she had no other choice. It was him or her, and her entire family. All this is quite consistent with the description given by my mother and explains her strong and impressive personality.

We know now that Pop Seddon's family came back twice from Australia to Poigny-la-Foret and visited Hotel "Au Petit Paris". Pop did not want to come back himself but his wife and daughters did.

My parents were also in direct contact with Maurice Cherbonnier's family in Chevreuse. In the Comet Line network we had for sure François Prompsaud (Rambouillet), Gaston Baillon (Gazeran) bringing food, and Mrs. Angélique Bie (Poigny La Foret) convenient Hotel to hide airmen in the country.

For obvious safety reasons, the Resistance network was never mentioned, members knowing only the ones they had to know to relaying evasions. My parents never mentioned the Comet Line, they probably did not know the name.

We have found Anne-Marie's name quoted in several documents, she is identified by her code name Antoinette or Marie-Antoinette. The fact she had one blue eye and one brown eye, also mentioned by Bill Leishmann, is a rare proof that nobody can deny.

Mrs. Bie had been betrayed for helping aviators in a letter sent to the Gestapo in Rambouillet. The postman – in the underground too - opened the letter before delivering it and warned her. So, she had time to take out from the Hotel any evidence of aviators passing through.

Anne-Marie was there when the SS came to interrogate Angélique. She was sleeping in the hotel that evening, which she was doing from time to time, when it was too late for her to cycle back to St. Remy. Listening in the night to a loud discussion downstairs, she went down to see what it was about. She found the SS interrogating Mrs. Bie.

She then started to speak to the SS (she was not fluent in German) and probably mentioned to them the names of officers residing in her home.

At the end of the discussion in the night, the SS left the hotel giving recommendations to Mrs. Bie to avoid doing things which would give other people the idea she was helping airmen. These were really sad and hard times, people betraying for ten thousand francs. My father used to say, in every man, you can get the worst and the best, this is what war was revealing. It is quite easy to understand why people were not speaking at all.

Mrs. Angelique Bie sheltered seven airmen during the war, at the risk of her own life and family, and we know that it was a real danger, not a fancy risk. On one occasion, she brought back on her shoulders, a wounded airman, she was only five feet tall but strong in her heart and full of energy like Anne-Marie.

She was born in 1893 in St. Nom-la-Breteche, she was 51 in 1944. She also deserves our admiration and respect. She was decorated, by the USA, France and Great Britain, she probably, like many others, did not attach a great value to decorations, but she was doing what she thought was right, at a risky time. When you go on the battlefield, you never think you may be killed.

We know now that "Antoinette" participated, along with F. Prompsaud, in the transfer of P. Lamason and K. Chapman (dressed up as painters) to Rambouillet on June 14th and then to Chevreuse (dressed up as firemen) on July 5th with Maurice Cherbonnier.

Josselyne has also found a letter sent by Anne-Marie to Mr and Mrs. Baillon when General de Gaulle died in 1970. Letter begins with "My name was "Antoinette" in these times". (see Appendix 8). Another proof of what she was doing, even though she never told to her daughters that she had killed a man during the war.

Anne-Marie, as many others then, did not speak of what she did during the war. It is clear, in doing what she was doing, that she probably felt constantly insecure, the dog and the gun were probably great comfort to her, especially when she was cycling in forest at night. Nobody will ever know the circumstances which led her to kill a man, though the fact must certainly be true, this is not something you invent during a short meeting with airmen who had seen death passing close to them two days before.

The Anne-Marie Saville Library (courtesy of Marie-Pierre Saville).

Anne-Marie had also close contacts with J. J. Desoubrie who had infiltrated at least five or six Resistance networks. It's probably following a meeting she had with him on August 10th, 1944 near Porte d'Auteuil in Paris that she started to understand he was a traitor. He had tried to kill one of his mistresses, right after the meeting. His mistress had also understood he was a traitor. Having been exposed publicly, he fled to Germany before the end of August.

In October 1944 Anne-Marie was enroled by the Red Cross to take out the prisoners from Concentration camps in Germany, which she did until June 1945.

She married Philippe Cerf in November 1946, she had two daughters Geraldine in 1948 and Carlyne in 1950. Philippe had joined the FFL in 1943 in North Africa. He participated in 1944 in tough battles at Monte Cassino, at the landing in Provence and at the battle of the Belgian Ardennes in 1945. He was awarded the War Cross after landing in Provence, and the Légion d'Honneur a few months before his death.

Anne-Marie married Pierre Saville (Schumann) in 1958 and they had a third daughter, Marie-Pierre in 1959. Pierre Saville had joined early the General de Gaulle in London, passing through Gibraltar. He joined the 82nd Airborne Division soon after, a Division similar to the U.S. Green Berets.

He was parachuted into Normandy on June 5th, badly wounded and left on the ground as dead on June 6th. He survived, thanks to an old lady who took him from the battlefield. He has been decorated by France and the USA. Purple Heart, War Cross, Military Medal, and Légion d'Honneur from General de Gaulle in 1966.

An exceptional woman, with a great sensibility, Anne-Marie kept throughout her life a strong attachment to her values and her great faith. Her father was Catholic, her mother Orthodox, she had decided to be Protestant. Saint Paul's words describe accurately what her life was like. "I fought, I ended up my journey and I kept my Faith." She settled down in the south East of France in La Garde-Freinet where she built her home.

She had a natural gift for arts and culture, and remained very active throughout her life, participating in the life of her village without seeking to take any official role, but clearly engaged politically. She was for a while a decorator, an antiques store dealer and created a library in La Garde Freinet which bears her name.

A gifted woman of "great winds" as Geraldine loves to say, an outstanding cook, loving nature and animals, she had also a great sense of humor and great generosity. With her, things were moving fast, like with "Small Cyclone" Andrée de Jongh.

Like my parents and many others, she kept after the war close contacts with all friends who participated in combats with her or her husband. Such experiences create solid links which never disappear. Anne-Marie fought during her entire life all injustices with courage and lucidity.

Lise de Boucherville Baissac, from Mauritius, was one of her great friends, she was among the first women parachuted by SOE in France during the war, in occupied territories, at the age of 37. They seem to have had during the war, quite similar experiences.

Pierre Saville (Schumann) passed away in 1976 in Paris, following surgery.

Anne-Marie passed away in March 1984, after a long medical treatment that she faced with courage, at the age of 62. She now rests in peace, with her husband, in the Montparnasse Paris cemetery. Throughout her entire life, she had always been facing tough events.

"Faire Face" was the motto of Guynemer, another aviation WWI hero, and also the motto of the French Fighters Weapons School, "Salon De Provence". It summarises quite well the great person Anne-Marie was, as described by my mother and Bill Leishmann.

"I will never forget how efficient she was". May her memory be remembered and honoured as much as others.

Philippe Cerf passed away in 1990, he was awarded the Légion d'honneur decoration a few weeks before leaving us.

Lise Baissac passed away twenty years after her friend Anne-Marie in March 2004, she was about to be 99 years old. She was certainly another strong character, having faced extreme frightful situations throughout her life.

The following anecdote illustrates the woman of exception she was. A few years after the end of the war, she was attending a conference in UK about SOE operations during the war. The speaker explaining SOE[25] operations in France mentioned the fact that one night, right after having been parachuted somewhere in France, he had made love to a woman but never had a chance to know who she was .

Lise Baissac then asked publicly the question "Do you remember the date and the location?" The speaker answered right away.

"Do you remember the hour?" she then asked.

"About four o'clock in the morning," he replied. Then Lise stood up and declared, "It was me!"

---

[25] SOE. "Special Operations Executive". English secret organisation, independent of MI5, 6, and 9. Created in 1940 by Churchill to assist the Resistance in occupied territories and supporting actions in spying, sabotage and reconnaissance by parachuting in equipment and agents. One of their networks was infiltrated for several months by the Germans in The Netherlands. A major victory for SOE was to destroy in 1944 the stock of "Heavy Water" in Norway with the help of a few dozen Norwegians trained in Scotland. They prevented the Germans from making the Atomic Bomb a few months later and undoubtedly changed the course of war. General de Gaulle did not much like SOE because they conducted their attacks in France without keeping him informed, even though throughout the war SOE gave strong support to the Underground.

Resistance and Liberation in La Celle-Les-Bordes

Let's go back now to the Resistance during the war in the Chevreuse valley. There were not many large battles around, the life in the village was rather quiet during the "Occupation". Many Paris area inhabitants were coming to get some food or live there, mainly during the later part of the war. Most of the villagers did not suffer too much of the lack of food supply because everybody developed family gardens, breeding chicken, rabbits, pigs, which were mainly a substitute. The Public School was opened normally.

There were quite often aircraft dog fights above the county, a kind of routine, with bullets whistling around. One day, André Billard living in Les-Bordes was witness to such a fight between German planes and English ones, easily identified by differences in colour and black crosses. That day, a German plane was shot down by an English one in front of them, children applauded, forgetting the German soldier near by witnessing the same fight. Nicely enough, the German soldier did not say anything.

My brother and sister told me when they were walking to La Noue farm to get milk, at about a distance of one mile, it happened several times they had to lie down in the ditch, listening to the whistles of bullets falling around. It was not a good way to protect themselves but they had learnt a bullet that you hear is not dangerous, it means it passes near by.

I have listed about a dozen planes which crashed around, mainly in the forest. As a child, I gathered unexploded ammunition coming from the wrecks, when I was walking in the woods, quite a dangerous exercise. I would recover the powder inside cartridges to make nice fires, without saying anything to my parents.

German pilots, when killed in the crash, were simply buried nearby in the forest, with a simple wooden cross, painted in kaki green.

Survivors were arriving quite regularly in the area – probably several hundred during the war - a support line had spontaneously been put in place to ease their escape.

Allied fighters had often additional fuel tanks that they dropped before engaging in the fights, to keep good maneuverability against German planes. It is another childhood memory. There were five or six of these rusted tanks which had been stored in front of the Town hall, in a line a few yards long. They had been recovered with great care by the population, there was some gasoline left inside in arriving on the ground, a rare product during war. It was the same for airmens' parachutes, which were used to make good quality shirts…

On August 26th and 28th 1944, a local Liberation Committee was settled with the following Resistance Groups identified and represented as follows in Town Hall registers.

Group Libération	Mr Maurice Dacheux,
Group Libération Vengeance	Mr Eugène Blin,
Group Résistance	Mr Maurice Flanchet,
Group Front National	Mr Firmin Tondeur,
Group SFIO party	Mr Achille Porcheron,
Group Radical Socialist party	Mr Désiré Boule,
Group Christian Democrats	Mr Albert Thirouin,
Group représenting War Prisoners Germany)	Mr Roland Vallet (prisoner in

The bureau elected the following members.

President	Mr Albert Thirouin
Vice President	Mr Désiré Boule
Secrétary	Mr Eugène Blin, representing the FFI
By superior order	

On September 7th, 1944, this local committee was the only legal power in the county, with a few seats being vacant, in case new Resistance movements would show up to be recognised .

Such a reserve clearly illustrates the politician's strategy to take over the control including some people who did not take any risk during the war. The same procedure was in place in surrounding counties.

I understand better now the thoughts my parents had about the people they called "The last hour fighters" when FFL groups appeared in 1944 with loud public demonstrations they did not approve. Mr François

Prompsaud, another Comet Line hero from Rambouillet, declared exactly the same thing.

On September 11th, following a letter dated September 4th, coming from the President of Department Liberation Committee, the Committee suspended the Mayor elected in 1938, Mr Eugene Caujolle and named in his place Mr Albert Thiroin on the pretext that he had attended a football match with German players and he had not installed the Supply Commissions approved by the assistant to the Prefect which had been put at his disposal.

These motives look quite weak and questionable, when you put them in perspective. Great disorder was reigning all around. They did not prevent Mr Caujolle from being re-elected Mayor in 1947. For obvious reasons I knew quite well the small group of Resistants dealing with my parents during the war. The names of those I remember are listed herebelow, there were certainly a few others.

The priest for the village and Clairefontaine. Fidèle François Joseph Gallazzini. He had lunch or dinner at our home every week and I am named François after him. A saint, according to what my mother said, he gave to others everything he was given. This is the reason why he was invited to our home once a week to be sure he would have some decent food from time to time. He died in 1947. I remember him very well.

The bookseller in Chevreuse, Maurice Cherbonnier, and his family. Maurice belonged to the Comet network and had also been in contact with the OSS and the SOE. He was given the credit for helping 21 airmen escape; they were lodged in the top floor of his house, an operation which was quite risky, in so far as they were in the centre of the town. He owned a radio transmitter to communicate with the Intelligence Service.

He had a Briard dog "Marette" who barked whenever the German "Gonio[26]" car was approaching He would stop transmission immediately and was never detected by the Germans. The airmen were somewhat like lions in a cage, when they were hidden and his wife Thérèse had sometimes trouble keeping them quiet and not making too much noise which could be heard in the street.

---

[26] Vehicle equipped with a radiogoniometry detector to pinpoint the location of wireless transmitters.

Janine, their daughter married in 1947 an English RAF airman, Harry Sanderson. At the end of the war, he was working in SHAPE, in Rocquencourt, and came during the week ends as an Airman family support, just as Ellen Grant Dalton was inviting Ken Bryan at home.

The "family doctor" in Chevreuse, Doctor de Palma and family. He and his wife Janine lived in a house on the main street in Chevreuse. He took care of wounded aviators as needed, as well as Doctor Dugue and pharmacist Grish, who also lived in Chevreuse.

Our neighbours, in la Villeneuve, the Proix/Birdsall family. Their house in La Villeneuve had probably been bought in the thirties. Marthe Proix went to London in 1940 with her daughter Genevieve and the house was looked after by Mr Olivier during the war. It had been used for a while for his family when a Focke Wulf 190 crashed between the two houses on August 16th 1944 and set on fire his own house, which was entirely destroyed except for the stone walls.

Mrs. Marthe Pauline Noe, widow of Pierre Proix, was an Engineer graduated from University in the twenties, quite rare at the time for a woman. She was born on April 15th, 1897 and was living in Neuilly, Avenue du Roule. She went to London in 1940 with her daughter Genevieve who served in either the WAAF (Women Auxiliary Air Force) or WRNS (Women's Royal Naval Service) and after the war, the Secret Service. Their house in La Celle-les-Bordes, in La Villeneuve hamlet, was a week-end house.

We were living in the County Town Hall School "Mairie - Ecole", on a hill side between the two villages of La Celle and Les-Bordes, in the woods. The location of the building had been selected in the previous century on the hill side not to give a preference to one of the two villages.

The building was surrounded by thirty metre high pine trees "Piceas". They had grown throughout years and were casting their shadow on the building during the day. So Classrooms were quite dark and lacked light. It took about ten years for my mother to get the Mayor and the Council to cut down these four high pine trees.

My father was a Town Hall secretary, my parents were both teachers.

The "Mairie – Ecole" building included.

Second floor: Attics,

First floor: Apartment for Teacher, Town hall conference room (right side) used for Council meetings, Weddings and Archives, my father's Office, Telephone exchange switchboard,

Ground floor: Two classes, on the left side (my father) children from 9 to 12, on the right side (my mother) young children from 5 to 8,

Basement: Cellar on left side, used during the war to store ammunition.

Mairie Ecole with flag and flower beds prepared for a wedding ceremony (author's photo).

When an airman landed in the area, he was sheltered from place to place by people belonging to the Underground network. For obvious safety reasons, people never spoke about this, as enemy ears could be everywhere.

In "Behind Enemy lines", the Canadian F/O. Bill Leishman, Navigator of Australian P/O Pop Seddon crew speaks about FFL demonstrations in the streets, public trials of women having had relations with Germans being jailed by the police for their protection. A document published recently mentions – even though reliable statistics do not exist – that about 200,000 children were born with a German father. And the same occured in Germany with prisoners and STO workers. It is clear that the situation must have been quite confused in 1944 when the Germans left.

There was a nice tradition in La Celle-les-Bordes for weddings at that time; School children were making in front of Town Hall an alley with two lines of flower beds in the sand with kids kneeling behind. When the guests to the wedding go out of Town Hall, they would drop coins on the flower beds, the nicest obviously better rewarded than the others. Children were having great discussions afterwards counting the respective amounts they collected.

The French flag floated during the entire war in front of the building where I was born. The first thing the Germans did when they arrived in Paris had been to put a huge German flag on the Eiffel tower. Soon after they occupied the area, an SS officer came and ordered my father to remove the French flag hanging above the entrance door.

My father then argued with the SS officer. "Think about it, the Town Hall building is two hundred yards from the road in the woods, nobody can see it from the road. If we don't leave a distinctive sign in front of the building, nobody will ever know and find where Town Hall is located." The SS officer accepted the explanation and confirmed his agreement to leaving the flag where it was.

This agreement was used thereafter as an alibi during the entire war for all other Germans passing around and asking for it to be taken down. In quite a number of cases, the Germans were saluting the flag before leaving, which made my father - a Captain in French army - happy and laughing.

A number of Parisians who came to visit La Celle-les-Bordes during the war, could not believe it, but the facts are documented in the county legal books. My parents have always declared having had correct but cold relations with the Germans during the "Occupation" of French territory. Some Germans (not the SS) were there without having been given the choice and they did not necessarily like it too much.

One day, a plane having been shot down above the village, the pilot having baled out safely, an SS officer visited the Town Hall seeking information and asking if somebody had seen the pilot. In fact, the pilot who had landed not far away, was temporarily hidden in the attic, waiting for another more discreet place. My father answered negatively, of course. A farmer, who was there to settle an administrative problem when the SS arrived, said, "It's normal that the pilot hides himself, after all, that's his job."

The German officer, coldly scolding the farmer, said to him, "No Sir, he is not doing his job, he is doing his duty."

On several occasions my parents had hidden people during the war at home, Town Hall status giving a neutral but risky protection. There were many visitors, and absolute discretion was a must, with panels threatening airmen helpers displayed in front of the building.

My father, as Town Hall secretary, among other things, was responsible for distributing food rationning tickets to the population. It was easy for him, to deliver food to airmen passing through. One day, he gave food tickets illegally to an old person lacking food in the village. Immediately afterwards the man betrayed him for illegal practice and received money from the Gestapo.

My father was then summoned by the Kries Kommandantur in Ramboullet to explain what he was doing (they for sure, were investigating for food tickets given to airmen). My mother, telling the story said, "When he left in the morning, I did not know if he would be back in the evening."

He had put on his captain uniform and was lucky enough to meet a Lieutenant from Prussia in Rambouillet who did not appreciate Nazism too much. When my father entered the office, the German Lieutenant stood up and saluted my father. Then he told him the true story, and said to my father how much the Gestapo had paid to get the information.

My father then said to the German, "What would have you done yourself, seeing a poor man starving to death?" And he came back free in the evening. It was war, end of story.

My father used to say, "In every man, you can find the worst and the best, a totally lost case does not exist." To explain and support his saying, he occasionally explained what happened to him during WWI on the battlefield. Being an officer, he had an assistant, an "aide de camp". The man was in fact a murderer, jailed before the beginning of war, he had been taken out from prison to go on the battlefield. Nobody else wanted to use the services of the man, but my father did.

He said to him, "I don't want to know anything about what you've done in the past. This is what I am expecting from you now and if you do it, you will never have any problem with me and others, as long as I am around."

Some time after, on the battlefield this man, seeing a German aiming at my father, stood up in front of him and was killed in his place. A murderer had saved another's life.

Living conditions were not flourishing in the village, but when you live in the country and you are well organised, you suffer much less for food supply than those living in cities. My parents had started, like everybody, to breed chickens, rabbits, and even pigs. During the war, they were giving on a regular basis some food and flowers to their friends coming from Paris. I remember well the packs of eggs cautiously wrapped in a journal sheet and in season, large smelling lilac bouquets when they were leaving home.

My father had established three gardens near the school, each child from the age of 7, had his own square to plough. The soil was quite light and sandy but the ground is low and we learnt quickly the value of things, which did not kill us for sure.

My mother had great memories of the US army passing through the area. The soldiers where distributing chewing gum, chocolate, coffee, concentrated milk, goods quite rare at the time. She could not sleep the first night after she drank real coffee again. It had been replaced by chicory since 1940.

I am just trying to describe the ambiance and how life was organised in the village. Human solidarity was everywhere, people helping each other but never saying a word about what they were doing in the underground, safety rules were observed first. The country was occupied, every day events were a reminder to the population that enemy ears could be everywhere, you had to mistrust everybody around.

I found in legal registers of the Town council, the first mentions about the FFI in August 1944. The groupment "Vengeance" – Revenge – had been created in St.Cyr-sous-Dourdan in 1940, then transfered to Dourdan soon after. They actively participated in many sabotage actions in the area, sanctioned by German deadly retaliation actions in surrounding cities. German reprisals left behind traces hard to wipe out, like the story of Jo's father, who had been arrested tortured and deported to Buchenwald, where he died. Josselyne has never been able to trace the circumstances of his death. Life had to go on, people did not have any other choice.

A report published for the Prefect in Rambouillet in August 1944 testifies the village had relatively not suffered too much during the war, apart from some isolated cases of combats in the area. It confirms also that the Occupants had in general a correct behavior during the war.

When you analyse the betrayal which led to John Clarke and many others' arrest, it all started with infiltration of Resistance networks by a double agent, Jacques Desoubrie. This man obviously got a significant amount of money from the Gestapo. He had a really troubled life, but he had been smart enough to get the confidence of many Resistance members, justified by terrorist actions he claimed to have performed, probably sometimes invented with the help of the Gestapo.

He was using four different identities in several areas, he had several mistresses, sometimes he managed to get rid of their husband when they were married, by having the husband arrested, a real "salaud".

As mentioned before, Anne-Marie de Dudzeele probably started to realise he was a traitor with the arrest of airman E. Jackson on August 10th 1944, when he tried to kill his mistress.

E. Jackson's testimony was produced during the trial of J Desoubrie in 1949. Josselyne Pichon has cautiously documented his full story in her research, they leave no room for interpretation about the role he played and what he did during the war.

Watching the fast US Army progress inside France after D-Day, and realising it would not take too long before he was discovered, he was risking great problems with the FFI . He fled to Germany around 20th August 1944 , just a few days before Paris liberation by General LeClerc.

On May 17th, 1945 E. Jackson wrote a letter produced during his trial to testify about Jean Jacques Desoubrie's treachery.
We'll come back later to this traitor, caught up by the US army in 1947 in Germany and brought back to France to attend his trial.

Liberation of Chevreuse by US Army in August 1944

Anne-Marie with her sister Hélène and her father Count Gaston Errembault de Dudzeele (courtesy of Geraldine Cerf de Dudzeele).

The Germans had a strong motivation to prevent airmen from making it back to England to pursue re-engagment with the RAF. Resistants who were arrested for helping aviators or for any other reason, common practice was to torture them. The Gestapo was extracting its revenge for those betrayals.

One can't question the high risks Resistance members were taking for their own life, for doing what they were doing during war. In addition to networks infiltrated by the Germans, airmen when they were caught, could speak about the places they had been through in their escape, not necessarily under constraint, and then could help to identify their helpers. This is how the Dassie family had been identified in Bayonne.

You then come to a new question. Why my parents, who were throughout the war in the chain of airmen escapes, were not identified by the Gestapo? According to Jo, who never met Maurice Cherbonnier, on several occasions Maurice had been about to be arrested in traps organised by Germans, but he managed to escape each time with good explanations proving his good faith. He was living dangerously.

Josselyne Lejeune-Pichon gave me also another good explanation. For Jean Jacques Desoubrie, not saying too many things about people on the ground was for him a good way to preserve his revenues coming from the Germans and a sordid way to protect his business.

You may then ask the same question on the Gestapo side. Letting Resistance members on the ground continue to act was also a good way to be sure to catch them before they took the train to the South west of France. The only important point for the Gestapo was to prevent them from getting airmen back to the UK.

Retrospectively, it is frightful that the risks people were taking in the field were real ones. I never had this discussion with my parents, I am sure they were fully aware of their situation. They had the same motivations as airmen, to fight the Nazis whatever happened. I don't think they would have changed anything to what they were doing if they had been aware of Desoubrie's dealings.

Dedee said the same thing to all those joining the Comet Line; "With me, you won't last more than six months, it's the average." The only question was not if they would be arrested, but when. The remarkable thing is to notice that the ones who survived, after having been through horrible experiences, facing things like torture and deportation, all say the same thing: "If I had to do it all again, I would."

The occupiers' repressive actions sometimes incited population to perform violent actions. War breeds war. One day, the father of my classmate, Paul Poisson, had obtained some weapons somewhere and he was willing to organise an attack against the Germans in the county.

It happens that my father had been his Captain in the French Army in 1939, living in the same village creates links. So he went to see my father, explaining to him his project. My father dissuaded him from doing anything. "There is such an imbalance in strength between us and the Germans, at the best you will kill a few Germans, but you are sure to be killed in return, along with a few other innocent people." Mr Poisson kept his weapons hidden during the war.

On August 14th there was an unexplained bombing performed by US or English planes in the South of La Villeneuve in the afternoon. It caused a fire in the forest which propagated to about fifty acres. The fire was extending more due to unexploded ammunition and dried brackens in the forest than with bombs themselves. La Celle County and Clairefontaine firemen departments helped by villagers managed to stop the fire by the end of afternoon.

Unfortunately, a woodcutter Mr R. Fourny was wounded in the back by ammunition exploding spontaneously in the forest with the fires. He was transported to the Rambouillet hospital, but his condition was not too worrying. At around 9.00 pm, the fire started again in the forest on about one hundred acres, fought by firemen and the population until dawn.

On August 15th 1944, at around 13.00 pm another bombing aiming at an artillery convoy moving in the area occured. A great dogfight followed between two dozen Focke Wulf 190s and seven US P47. Four Focke Wulf and three P47 were shot down during the fight, one of them crashed near La Villeneuve hamlet. The US pilot, 1st Lt William Buttner, was killed when his plane crashed in flames, without causing any other casualty, about 150 yards from Carrefour Verneuil and three hundred yards from Mrs. Proix and Olivier's family houses.

1st Lt William Buttner was buried on August 17th in La Celle cemetery beside his RAF comrades, next to the grave of Robert C. Guy, initially as an unknown airman, his dog tag having not been found among the debris of the plane. The plane, however had been clearly identified as an American one, with inscriptions found on parts, as mentioned in the civil Register.

These days had been quite busy in La Celle with fires in the forest, bombings and dogfights. They raised up to about ten or twelve the number of planes shot down during the war in La Celle-les-Bordes County as previously mentioned, including at least six FW 190s, one Lancaster and two P47 Razorbacks.

1st Lt. W. M. Buttner and F. Gabreski's P47 Thunderbolt 275510, A - HV shot down in La Villeneuve (courtesy of Air Museum Seattle).

William M. Buttner

1st Lt. W. M. Buttner (courtesy of Paul Stouffer)

The four Focke Wulfs shot down crashed in the forest surrounding La Celle, one beside the Bois du Roi (not far from the place the tail of the Lancaster fell) and three near the "Parc de la Verrerie" (probably near the place the nose of the Lancaster crashed). German pilots, when they died in the crash were buried in the forest near the wreck with a simple wooden cross painted in kaki green. I remember very well three of them.

The second American pilot managed to bale out of his plane and landed near the "Carrefour Peronnelle"and the Chêne Quinquet track. He was first hidden by a forest guard, but since he was wounded with a broken arm and several shrapnel fragments in his

145

body, he was taken by the Germans who probably drove him to hospital in Rambouillet, like Mr Fourny.

On August 15th several fires in the forest had reactivated in the evening, on a three hundred acre surface. Fortunately, a storm occured at around 9 pm, and rain eased their extinction.

When the US Army advanced through the area they freed William on August 28th and he was admitted in the 77th Evacuations Hospital. He was transfered back to the USA soon after. A medical report refers to the Fletcher General Hospital in Cambridge (Ohio) on September 3rd, 1944 and convalescence in Fort George Wright hospital (Washington DC) on January 30th 1945.

2nd Lt. William R. Sheppard, 1943 (courtesy of Bill Sheppard).

William probably met his wife in Cambridge when he was convalescent, this is destiny. La Celle-les-Bordes register mentions he had immediately been taken by US army passing through, which is inaccurate and shows how difficult it is sometimes, to establish historical truth even with official archives.

The third P47 pilot shot down the same day in Clairefontaine is the Captain Everett G. King, born in 1920. He baled out too, but unfortunately, his parachute did not open correctly in torchlight and he was killed upon arriving on the ground. Ydoine Riviere witnessed Everett King's accident with his parachute in torchlight, one hundred yards in front of her. Everett was buried the next day in a temporary grave on August 16th 1944 in Clairefontaine by the priest F. Gallazzini. Jean Louis and Ydoine Riviere attended the ceremony.

War Theatre #12 (England) CREWS - Fighter   4x5 neg rec'd 2/16/44 from RPR to accompany
                                              Press Release "TRIPLE THREAT." (1 photo)
                                       (over)

Lt Colonel Gabby Gabreski is congratulated on his promotion at the age of 25, January 30th, 1944. The painted swastikas display the number of victories claimed by the plane's pilots.

The three P47 came from the same squadron, based in Normandy in Tour-En-Bessin where a new airport had been installed at the end of July 1944. They belonged to the 373rd Fighter Group, which was part of the 9th Air Force.

Once again, our thanks go to Serge Querard, Jean Huon and Thierry Boche who had contacted him. Thanks to them, we have been able to trace the three American families who brought up key information about the three USAAF airmen shot down on August 15th, 1944.

- Paul Stouffer, nephew of 2nd Lt William J Mc Gowan, shot down on June 6th 1944,
- Robert Carmody, cousin of 1st Lt William M Buttner, shot down on August 15th 1944
- Bill Sheppard, son of 2nd Lt William Sheppard, shot down on August 15th 1944

The two P47 pilots – McGowan and Buttner – had graduated from the same advanced P47 school of Harding Field (Louisiana). They had received their wings at about the same time in December 1943 and January 1944 respectively. William Sheppard had been trained in Spence Field (Moultrie) Georgia in 1943 and transferred to Europe in 1944.

We know now, thanks to Paul Stouffer, that 1st Lt. W. Buttner P47 – 42 75-5510 – HV had been before the plane of Francis (Gabby) Gabreski, the greatest USAAF hero of WW II and Korea with 34.5 victories registered on P47 (28) and Sabre F 104 (6.5).

The P47 that crashed in La Villeneuve had 11 victory swastikas painted on the fuselage when she was shot down above La Celle-les-Bordes.

Thierry Boche found dozens of parts of the plane and forwarded some of them to the Air Space National Museum in Seattle for identification, where Paul Stouffer found the P47 picture shown above. It is the same for 2nd Lt. W. Sheppard P47 crash site, accurately described in La Celle-les-Bordes registers, metallic parts are still there in the forest.

Francis (Gabby) Gabreski had just celebrated his 25th anniversary when he was promoted to the rank of Lt. Colonel, the day he claimed his 11th victory in January 1944. A survivor in 1941 of Japanese bombings in Hawai, he had been held prisoner by the Germans the day of his last victory in Europe and eventually transferred in Stalag Luft I camp where F/S Stanley Hope, F/S William Greave, F/S George Ross and P/O Lyndon Lewis had been assigned.

1st Lt. W. M. Buttner grave was transferred on August 31st 1945 to Solers US military cemetery (Seine et Marne). William originated from Twin Falls (Idaho), that's where his mother was living, and where his grave was eventually transferred back.

Planes shot down in the area did not account for any civilian victims, only one plane fell down on a house in La Villeneuve on August 16th 1944, a Focke Wulf 190 shot down during another dog fight. The pilot had been able to bale out before and was certainly recuperated by the German army. The plane in crashing set on fire the house of Mr Lucien Olivier, without hurting anybody, fortunately enough.

Wreckage of a Focke Wulf 190 shot down on August 16th, 1944 at La Villeneuve. From L to R. Simone, Lucie, Marcelle, Lucien Olivier and Robert, Paul Touny (courtesy of Simone Olivier).

Mrs. Marcelle Olivier, pregnant at the time, had had time to take refuge in a trench at the end of their garden with her four children. Lucien was helping firemen fighting the fires in the forest. He ran back home, thinking the German plane had crashed not far from his home. With three planes having crashed around in two days within a five hundred yards radius circle, the villagers must certainly have been upset.

On August 20th, eight US tanks crossed the village and went straight to Cernay la Ville. Temporarily, Lucien Olivier family settled down in Mrs. Proix's house near by. Lucien was looking after the house in the absence of the owner, Mrs. Marthe Proix when she was in London. Ruins of their house

June 8th 1945. Jacky Mercier, Simone and Lucie Olivier, unknown, Andrée Ydier behind Robert C Guy's grave. 1st Lt. W. M. Buttner's grave, to the left of my sister Andree, was transferred on August 31st 1945 to Solers US cemetery (author's photo).

(stone walls) are still there, the wreck of FW 190 was removed a few years ago.

Lucien Olivier and his family then settled down in "Pavillon des Gaules", near the church and La Cellecastle. Thanks to my research on the DS822 and Serge Querard, I have also found the Nanny who was taking care of me after the war. Mrs. Simone Olivier (Petit), she had ended Primary school and passed successfuly the "Certificat d'Etudes" in 1946. As André Billard is saying, she loved young kids.

End of the War and the Post War Period

Coming back to a normal life at the end of conflicts has not always been easy for heroes having lived in permanent stress for several years. Many of them never succeeded in re-adapting to a civilian life. Thank God, it has not been the case for our friends. Let's see the continuation of their story, following the same order as before.

P/O Jack A.N. Durham

In July 1943 Archibald had married an English girl, Joan Henderson from Newcastle, who was a WAAF (*) at Waterbeach. Jack left the RAF in October 1945, I did not find additional combat missions in archives between September 1944 and his departure for Australia the following year. He probably flew from the UK to Australia and was discharged from the RAAF soon after his return in November 1945.

Joan and Jack had a son, Donald Norman, born in Newcastle in November 1945. As a consequence, she waited a few months before going back to Australia. She travelled in a ship, the "Highland Princess" which left Liverpool on March 26th 1946 for Sydney, where she arrived in April 1946.

Jack had been promoted in the RAAF to Pilot Officer rank, backdated to May 14th 1944 which probably explains the error made by a journalist in Australia, about the function A.N. Durham had on board the DS822 Lancaster, that I mentioned already.

Jack was discharged on Oct 4th, 1945 from the RAAF in the rank of Flying Officer. Through Veterans Associations, Kenneth Wright has been able to find traces of Joan and Archibald in Australia after their return and to establish the fact they both passed away in Brisbane suburbs, in an area named Chapel Hill, in the nineties. Kenneth is also in contact now with his younger brother James.

Upon his return to Australia, Archibald came back to his former employment as an accountant. As many others, he did not talk much about the war and did not show a great interest in Airmen Associations. However he remained active in the social area and received an MBE[27] for his

---

[27] Member of the Order of the British Empire

achievements in Assistance given to the Blind. He was a good Tennis player and later Lawn Bowls. Jack and Joan had only one son, Donald, born in Newcastle in 1945 as we know. He was killed in a tragic road accident at the age of 21 in 1966.

On the other hand and totally by chance, I made an interesting discovery. I found a "magic line" in the USA which impressively summarises their life. The following five cities in USA are almost perfectly aligned.

City	State	Straight Line Distance miles
Lancaster	South Carolina	-
Chapel Hill	North Carolina	128
Durham	North Carolina	10
Henderson	North Carolina	38
Lancaster	Virginia	152

I have not found elsewhere five other cities with the same names aligned like that in the world. It does not mean anything, of course, but it summarises pretty well the history of A.N. Durham's family. The funny thing is the way it was found, totally by chance without searching. How could you search for such an alignment without knowing the result in advance? Another coincidence in our history.

In the same vein, but for fun this time, Roger Guernon who has been a great contributor to our research was born on June 7th, the day our Lancaster left from Waterbeach. Another US P38 pilot, R.J. Gignac was shot down in Voisin-le-Bretonneux on June 7th. Roger was also able to trace his family for the Choisel exhibit.

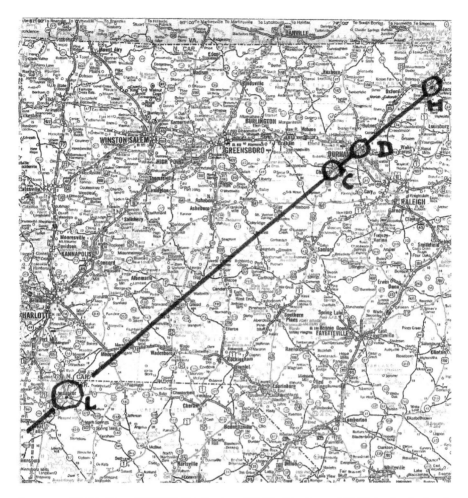

Lancaster SC (L), Chapel Hill NC (C), Durham NC (D), Henderson NC (H) (author's photo).

F/S John Clarke

John Clarke was discharged from the RAF on September 10th, 1946. He went back to live in his native city Coalville, and took over another job in NCB, the National Coal Board, in the payroll department. Four years later he married Daisy Clarke, the daughter of another NCB employee.

They had a son, Graham, in 1956 followed two years later by a daughter, Gillian Elisabeth. They were living at the time in a large Victorian house with a terrace until February 1964. They moved then to a modern house, in Coalville suburbs, wher Rachel Anne was born in 1964.

Stan Kershaw met John Clarke in 1991 and put him in contact with John Tanney who was also working in the Mine, after he met him in Ashington.

In 1993, John Clarke visited with Daisy and friends living in France in company of John Tanney La Celle-les-Bordes, to pay a tribute in the cemetery to their comrades.

John was also an active man, having always something to do. Throughout his entire life, he has been an active member of the Scout group Baden Powell and for years, was the leader of the first troup of Ravenstone. He was also the Treasurer of the local branch of the Royal British Legion.

John retired in 1990, after forty years of service in the National Coal Board. He then pursued his activities, as an active volunteer of MENCAP association, driving a Minibus, editing a local Paper, and helping for the delivery of meals in the area. If we summarise, John Clarke gave a lot to others during his entire life, during the war and in his civilian life, his children are very proud of his accomplishments, he deserves their pride.

F/S John Tanney

John lost his aptitude to fly in combat operations in March 1945, but he kept his qualification of Gunner. He participated in some missions over France, Germany, Spain and Portugal. In June 1945 the war had ended, so he attended a training session to become a cook in Blackpool. He then went to Bombay (Mumbai), Madras (Chennai) and Shanghai on board a ship passing through the Suez Canal. He came back to England on December 23rd 1946 and was discharged from the RAF in March 1947.

John decided then to go back to work in the Mine, where he was working before the war and he kept his job until he had to stop for health reasons. John was an active man, he loved gardening and long walks in the country.

John Tanney (left) and John Clarke at St. John's church, Waterbeach, for the 1995 annual reunion of 514 Squadron veterans (courtesy of Stan Kershaw).

The Boy and the Bomber

The Boy and the Bomber

P/O Lyndon Lewis

Lyndon when coming back from captivity in England, pursued his career with the RAF and Air Police. As his son Clive says, the farm hand, by order of the King, had become "an Officer and a Gentleman". In 1949, he was sent to Ismailia, in Egypt, in the Suez Canal area. The Suez Canal crisis was building up on the horizon, when he was repatriated to England, at Netheravon. That's where Geraldine was born, their fourth child.

Promoted to Squadron leader grade, he was transferred to Munchengladbach in Germany, then back again to England, working in the Air Ministry in London, 1956. That's when Lyndon joined the Freemasons for a long and happy period of time, in the Lodge Lux in Tenebris, on September 27th, 1957.

In 1960, he was promoted to Wing Commander and was posted to Singapore, where among other responsibilities, he was the President of the Officers's Club. He had then several appointments in England, in Littlegate and Gloucestershire where he retired in 1968.

During all those years, Lyndon was working for MI5, which explains why we were unable to find anything in the Archives. In 1979, he suffered the pain of losing, within a year, his daughter Jennifer following a long illness and his wife Margaret in a car accident, five months later.

Happily enough, the first daughter of Geraldine arrived soon after. In 1982 he had met Agnes, during a trip in Portugal. They decided to get married on April 10th 1982 and they spent a few happy years together, spending most of the winter playing golf in Spain and Portugal.

Agnes, a doctor, retired in 1991. In 1999, Lyndon had bowel cancer and the major surgery which followed, partially handicapped him. Agnes with the competence of a doctor, greatly helped Lyndon to overcome the problems the handicap brought, though he was still able to play golf.

Overall, putting everything in perspective, Lyndon had quite a busy life. He was lucky enough to meet two exceptional ladies Peg and Agnes. A strong and powerful personnality, physically and mentally, a true rock on which everybody could lean, loving life and fully enjoying life, as husband, father, grand father and great grand father.

In Freemasonry there is a saying, "If you rise to eminence by merit you will live respected and die regretted." Lyndon did live respected and died in 2006 regretted at the age of 90, like Andree De Jongh.

F/O William Lachlan McGown

William Mc Gown was promoted to Flying Officer on September 30th 1944. In accordance with procedure for security reasons, having been shot down in an occupied territory, he changed squadrons and went from 514 to 123 Squadron. Until the last day of his RAFservice on 11th April 1946, he continued to fly the Mosquito, a faster plane with a crew of two. William was awarded the DFC[28] on November 28th, 1944 and a bar to his DFC in October 26th, 1945.

He had married to Margaret Lockart before the war, unfortunately they did not have any family. After the war he returned to being a bookseller in the bookstore he had in Glasgow and finally retired as a bookseller. He passed away on 9th January 1984 at the age of 70 at Inverclyde Hospital, Greenock Scotland.

Violet Reith remembers him very well, as a man calm and level-headed. He was certainly a good man, as he was with his crew. Being older by about ten years than the others, he was probably behaving with them like a father.

He probably knew, certainly by name, Walter Gibb, a Mosquito pilot like him. We have not been able to find if the two men met each other during their lives, however it is quite likely that they did.

In the fifties, William sent back all his decorations to the RAF, considering his country had not given proper recognition of Bomber Command for their accomplishments during the war and their level of sacrifice in implementing strategic bombings.

I fully agree with William, that nobody should ignore the facts. The number of civilians killed in Germany did not destroy the morale of Germans, nor wreck the military manufacturing infrastructure as both Churchill and Harris had anticipated. However I remain fully convinced that without the bombing campaign, which necessitated the diversion of

[28] DFC – Distinguished Flying Cross, the third highest award for RAF airmen showing gallantry in combat.

countless troops, aircraft, ammunition and guns from the front line to anti-aircraft defence duties, the Nazi regime would have had a fair chance to implement its programmes of genocide and domination.

Just imagine what would the world be like today if the Germans had achieved the production of nuclear weapons (they were on the way to achieving their programme, until the providential SOE intervention in Norway), their supersonic jet fighters (they were nearly there), their V1 and V2s missiles (they were there too) and their chemical weapons (they had shown their willingness to use these in the genocide of millions in their extermination camps).

We would be all probably speaking German today, if we were around to speak at all.

In June 2012 Queen Elizabeth II unveiled a monument in Green Park, London dedicated to the men and women who served in Bomber Command. It is particularly telling that the memorial was funded by public donations rather than the successive governments that had ignored the heroism and sacrifice of 125,000 airmen and women who were willing to give everything. When the world needed heroes, it was those who put their lives on the line that saved us, rather than the politicians.

William McGown can now rest in peace with his decorations, as well as Ellen Grant Dalton who financed the construction of "their" Memorial in "La Petite foret" in La Celle-les-Bordes.

Oberleutenant Major Walter Borchers

Borchers, who claimed DS822 on the night in question, was killed on March 5th, 1945 with his radio operator in a Junkers 88 G, in the Lubeck area, in the North of Altenburg, Denmark. Only his gunner managed to bale out. He had shot down that day two four-engined bombers, raising his claimed victories to 59, of which 43 were at night. The Mosquito pilot who shot him down is Walter Gibb, from Scotland (like William McGown.)

Walter Gibb

Walter had made after the war a brilliant career in Aviation. As chief test pilot of the Bristol Aeroplane Company in the fifties, he broke several altitude records in with a Canberra above 80,000 ft. My friend Serge Sireau remembers him when he was in Bristol, working on the Jaguar programme.

In the Seventies, Walter was working on the Concorde programme, he ended up his career as President of British Aerospace Australia in the early Eighties.

The Guy family

Colin visited La Celle-les-Bordes in 1946 to pay a tribute to his brother Bertie in La Celle cemetery. He went there with my father who took the picture which had no date and no name. Thanks to Roger Guernon and

Jean Ronald comparing this photo with other pictures, we have been able to find the name of the British soldier kneeling down by the grave as Colin Guy. The picture was taken most probably in June 1946 by my father.

Robert C. Guy had a twin brother Charlie, the F/S Charles M. Guy, MKII Engineer in 514 Squadron too. He was flying with F/L. Walter J. Chitty, RAAF and had crash landed with him upon their return from Nuremberg on March 31st as we said before, the same day P/O McGown landed in the fog running out of gas, near Sawbridgeworth.

F/L. W.E. Chitty had been injured. When released from hospital he formed a new crew with

Colin Guy, brother of Charles and Bertie, at the latter's grave in 1946 (author's photo)

F/S Charlie M. Guy, while F/S Robert C Guy replaced F/S John Tanney in McGown's crew.

Sadly, the F/S C.M. Guy and F/L. W.E. Chitty were killed on July 30th 1944. They were lost at sea during an attack on the Caen area involving 18 bombers of 514 Squadron. During this operation, two Lancasters collided in the clouds at around 08.00 am, a Lancaster MkI HK 558, from 75 (NZ) Squadron, skipper F/S C.G. Nairne RNZAF and a MkII, LL733, from 514 Squadron, the skipper being F/L W.E. Chitty.

159

Bombing altitude that day was about 2,000 ft and the base of clouds about 3,000 ft. Only one body has been found in the sea by a Royal Navy vessel, HMS Hannaray, patrolling below in the Channel,.
The body was identified as F/S C.G. Nairne from New Zealand. He was buried at sea the same day, according to maritime tradition. No trace of other the airmen has been found, they are all honoured in Runnymede Memorial.

Another coincidence was that on that very day, July 30th 1944, F/S Ross A. Flemming RCAF, a navigator with 514 Squadrn, flew his 32nd and last combat mission during the same Caen operation. His daughter is Wendy Flemming has done magnificent work over the years tracing veterans of the squadron and their families. We thank her sincerely for answering the many questions Roger Guernon and I had to help us in the research.

Jean Jacques Desoubrie

On the ground, J. J. Desoubrie had infiltrated five or six Resistance networks, in different areas with at least seven different names. He was certainly a shrewd and clever man, utilising his participation in real attempts or sabotage operations in the area to build the confidence of Resistants. Among the identities utilised, were Jean Masson, Pierre Boulain, Jacques Leman and J.J. Desoubrie.

He fled to Germany at the end of August 1944 when he thought with allied armies approaching Paris the atmosphere was about to be getting too hot for him... The US army caught him up in Augsburg on May 7th 1947, brought him back to France and put him in the hands of justice.

His trial took some time, the case was treated under four different jurisdctions, Lille, Douai, Angers and Paris associated to his different names. We don't know the exact number of the people he betrayed, certainly several hundreds. Some say 1,000 with 400 deportations, others speak of 130 Resistants and 150 airmen. It implies that he would have received from the Gestapo several hundred thousand euros at least.

He was sentenced to death on July 18th, 1949 in the Paris 8th Tribunal, Rue Boissy d'Anglas and shot in Montrouge Fort on December 20th, 1949 at 08.34 am. His last words were "Heil Hitler". One of his mistresses had been tried in May 1946 and acquitted due to lack of evidence. We will never know, this is the reason why I don't mention her name. At the beginning she was a true Resistance member and had been seduced and misleaded by J J Desoubrie like many others.

Proix / Birdsall family

My parents probably met Mrs. Marthe Proix and her daughter Genevieve before the war. They were living in Neuilly, Avenue du Roule and coming to La Celle-les-Bordes during the week ends. Genevieve was probably born around 1922. Mr Olivier living near by about 30 yards away, was looking after their house in their absence. Marthe Proix met Paul Birdsall during their staying in London.

Paul graduated from Harvard (1921), he had been a Teacher in History and Dean in Williams College (Massachussets). He had written a book, "Versailles Twenty Years After", explaining the 1919 Versailles treaty had almost caused WW II. He was an OSS[29] agent in London during the war. One of his student in Williams College, Hans Gatzke was German. Hans had decided not to go back to Germany and participate in the war. He was also enrolled by the OSS where his knowledge of German was useful.

At the end of war, Paul was working in London with General Eisenhower, he had the rank of Lieutenant Colonel in the US army. He had been appointed, Military attaché in the Paris US Embassy in 1946 and 1947, an important post, it was the beginning of the cold war. He went back to the USA in 1948/1949, in Brooking Institute, Washington DC, before joining the CIA later.

Geneviève Proix, Marthe's daughter was another great character, a ray of sunshine in our childhood. She had enrolled in the WAAF or the WRNS in London in 1940 and ended up the war in Secret Services, maybe OSS, activity she kept for a few years in the late forties.

She was making us dream when she was telling us how she was driving downstairs with her jeep. She had a German sheperd dog trained to kill - Rainco – frightening me, even though I like dogs. Paul Poisson remembers Rainco too. I remember Marthe quite well. I was a few years ahead at school, every time I was going to La Villeneuve, she was asking me

---

[29] OSS. Office of Strategic Services, predecessor of CIA, Central Intelligence Agency during WW II

Paul Birdsall and Marthe Proix's wedding at La Celle-les-Bordes on Saturday, October 11th 1947. Front row: Désiré Boule (Mayor) - Jeanne Boule, Andrée Ydier and Marguerite Tondeur seated baby Solange Tondeur. Back row: Firmin Tondeur (witness), Colonel Paul Birdsall, Ferdinand Ydier (witness), Marthe Birdsall / Proix, Hortense Longlune. Picture probably taken by Genevieve Proix (courtesy of Bernard Tondeur).

a thousand questions to check my knowledge, and every time I came back with pockets full of sweets, something that a kid remembers.

Fidele François Joseph Gallazzini

Born in 1903 in Algeria, he was Priest for Clairefontaine and La Celle-les-Bordes and was in the Underground network with my parents. His roots were from Corsica. He is the one who gave me my name, François and he put me under the protection of St François d'Assise.

SOUVENEZ - VOUS DANS VOS PRIÈRES
de

l'Abbé Fidèle François Joseph GALLAZZINI

né le 18 Mai 1903 à Miliana (Algérie)

ordonné prêtre à Casablanca le 29 Juin 1939

ancien Curé de Drocourt

Curé de Clairefontaine et de la Celle-Les-Bordes

retourné à Dieu le 21 Janvier 1947

dans la 44e année de son âge

et la 8e de son sacerdoce

MISÉRICORDIEUX SEIGNEUR JÉSUS, DONNEZ-LUI
LE REPOS ÉTERNEL.   (300 j. d'ind.)

'Remember in your prayers...' A memorial notice for priest Fidele Francois Joseph Gallazzini (courtesy of Ydoine Riviere).

He passed away on January 21st 1947. Somebody told me that, just before Fidèle died, there was somebody else close to him gravely sick and also dying. Fidèle said "Don't worry, he won't die." This is exactly what happened miraculously but he himself passed away a few days later, just as if he had given his own life.

The picture here below was given to me by Ydoine Riviere who knew him very well too, but did not know he was in the underground. André Billard who was a choir-boy, was moved when he saw the picture. He had also great memories of him and the motorcycle "Motobecane 125" he used for transport.

163

Cherbonnier Family

In the archives, we have found a document where Maurice declares he was in contact with an OSS agent, Commandant Laussuck, who was hidden in Paris in Mrs. Heraut's apartment, Orleans Avenue. I don't know if he had made the link with Paul Birdsall, but it is very likely they had met at some stage.

In January 1947, Janine Cherbonnier married Harry Sanderson. They had two children, Anne-Marie – "Pussy" - born in November 1947, Gerald - "Jerry" – born in March 1951.

In 1953, Janine became ill and doctors recommended that her child be taken out of their home. This is the reason why my parents kept Pussy for one year at home during the school period from September to June. I was quite often fighting with Pussy and my older brother Ferdinand was always taking her side, driving me crazy. Childhood stories.

Pussy was left handed, my mother taught her reading and writing with her right hand too. My father was also training us to write with the left hand too, saying "It maybe useful for you one day, you never know." In these years, my mother was sanctioned by her Academy Inspector because she refused to use the "Global method of reading", imposed by National Education Ministry. She was saying then, my mission is to teach children reading, writing and counting, when they leave me, they know how to read, write and count, I will not change my method, the analytical one.

You can smile today when you see the results in education with this harmful method, worse for French than English, with students at the end of secondary school having a level in spelling lower that the one we had at the age of ten. Surprisingly enough, this method, whose uselessness, in my opinion, has been demonstrated throughout the years (including by two Nobel Prize winners) continues to be applied in a more or less disguised form.

Josselyne Lejeune-Pichon, whose father had been deported to Buchenwald at about the same time as John Clarke, had found in archives information about Maurice Cherbonnier, whom she had never met. She was able to find the village "Beville Le Comte" near Chartres, where they retired and have their grave in the cemetery, where they rest in peace.

Thanks to Jo also, I have been able to find "Pussy" that I had been researching for a few years. On the same occasion, I learned with sadness that her mother Janine passed away in 1996, her grandmother Therese in 1998 and her brother Jerry in 2006.

Janine was a sweet blond pretty lady, whose voice sounds still in my memory. She had also participated actively in the Underground actions with her parents, she was about eighteen. According to Pussy, she had "an iron hand in a velvet glove", which is not surprising, you must have a strong character to do what she was doing at her young age. The father of Anne-Marie, Harry, passed away in 2008. May all their memories be also honoured for what they did during the war, we will remember them.

In 1947, my father was awarded the Légion d'Honneur for what he had done during the war. He received this decoration as a teacher, the first teacher in France to receive it, which caused some turbulence in the National Education Ministry.

He had before, like many others including Maurice Cherbonnier and Anne-Marie de Dudzeele, been recommended for other decorations like the War Cross and Military Medal, but he was not bothered. He used to say jokingly, there is only one cross I don't want to get, the wooden cross.

He had had the sad privilege in 1914 and 1939 to participate in two wars, WWI and WW II, had been held prisoner twice, and evaded twice. He was on the battlefield in Normandy in 1940 when he was held prisoner, he had two guns that he buried in a field before surrendering. a 1/3" Colt, 6 shots from 1914, and a 6.35 mm automatic gun, 12 shots from 1939. He came back at the end of war in Normandy to pick them up, they were a bit rusted but otherwise in quite a good condition on the whole.

In the late forties, without saying anything to my father, I was able to clean these guns and have them working back satisfactorily. I found ammunition in the Town Hall basement, then my brother and I went shooting with the guns I had repaired. Quite a number of deadly accidents happened in these years with kids, there was unexploded ammunition everywhere.

Cherbonnier, Birdsall, De Palma, Gallazzini, Proix, Countess of Montenegro and a few others; these are great names which I have kept in my heart from my childhood, I will never forget them and the stories they were telling us from time to time.

Another great memory from my childhood is seeing many airmen who came back revisiting their escape route in the early fifties. They all impressed me strongly, they were all speaking English and probably helped me to practice their language. As I said before, being ahead of schedule, I was taught Latin and English at the age of seven to keep me busy with Miss Gouineau in Versailles and my mother, so it was for me an excellent way to keep practicing.

Without any doubt, all these people were sharing with my parents the same values and I am proud to salute their memory and pay them the tribute they deserve for what they have done during the war. I do not think young generations can understand to day as we do, such feelings. It is in a way a good thing because we have not had since a global war like the one in 1940.

There is no good war for sure, we will never repeat that enough. However, it is important to remember and to stay aware of the price which was paid by all those brave men to conquer evil and provide the freedom we enjoy today. But we can never assume it will last for ever.

The Fifties and the Memorial in the Forest

As we have seen the years 1946/1947 had been rich ones with important miscellaneous events occuring to our friends .

1946 -Anne-Marie de Dudzeele's wedding to Philippe Cerf,
1946- F/S John Clarke and F/O W L McGown were discharged from the RAF,
1946- Proix/Birdsalls back in Paris.
1947- My father's Légion d'Honneur
1947- Sandersons' wedding, birth of Pussy 10 months later,
1947 -John Tanney was discharged from the RAF in March
1947- Proix/Birdsalls' wedding in October.

Let's go back to Ken Bryan's story, very well described by his young brother Neil Bryan. Neil wrote in the nineties a moving text, "My Brother Ken", entirely reproduced in Appendix 1 with his permission.

The custom, during the war, was that airmen from overseas were invited into homes of English families during their leave periods. Ken's English host family was Mrs. Ellen Grant Dalton, the widow of a Rear Admiral living in London and in the New Forest area, in Lyndhurst near Southampton.

Ellen was born in 1885, she was 59 in 1944, she had lost her husband in 1938. They had got married in 1915 and we think they had two children in 1916 and 1918. Ellen was an influent lady, living comfortably in London in Sloane Square, near Green Park with a chauffeur and a housemaid.

Ellen had an excellent education and spoke fluently French. She loved travelling. Her husband, a former Rear Admiral, became a diplomat when he left the Royal Navy. Ken was a few years younger than her sons, he was received in her home like a son. At that time, deer hunting in New Forest was a common practice, just like in La Celle-les-Bordes.

In the late forties, Ydoine Riviere sent a letter to Ken's parents, telling them what happened in June 1944 and that she had been able to contact Mrs. Grant Dalton. It's probably the reason why Ken's parents did not give their approval to the transfer of graves to a military cemetery. There was for a while some confusion about such a transfer, quickly settled by a RAF representative in 1946.

It is certainly the reason why the other two graves remained also in La Celle cemetery, contrary to other graves. 1st Lt W Buttner grave was transferred in August 1945, Atman Raba grave was transferred in the sixties, in presence of Jean Huon, the first writer of the DS822 story.

Ellen Grant Dalton came from London as soon as she could travel in the late forties to visit the place where Ken died in 1944. She then decided to have a Memorial built at her own expense and gave the project to her architect. The Memorial was built, probably in 1950, replacing the wooden cross which had been placed along the road D 61 before, between the two places where P/O Ken Bryan's and F/S George Boanson's bodies had been found in 1944.

On the Memorial (see picture page 35) you read that Ken Bryan is P/O (pilot officer) instead of W/O. (warrant officer) as mentioned in the RAF files, and that another unknown airman died in the crash, in addition to the three others.

P/O officer is the right rank, Ken having been promoted retroactively to the accident in May in Australia. In fact, the unknown airman never existed. The confusion came from the fact that F/S R.C. Guy's dog tag was not found in 1944. Bertie was buried first as an unknown airman. The Rear Gunner's name was confirmed later by a RAF representative F/Lt. Prior on February 27th, 1946 when he visited the cemetery with my father.

Neil Bryan says that he met Mrs. Grant Dalton in 1952, during a trip to Europe. This is the reason why he gave Ydoine's name to his daughter, a wish he made in the cemetery when he was with Ellen during his visit. Neil's daughter name, given a few years later, is Lisa Ydoine.

Neil had met Ellen in Paris. She took him to La Celle-les-Bordes and Clairefontaine where he met with Ydoine's parents in law. Ydoine had already gone with her husband Jean Louis to Brazil at the time, that's when Neil realised Ellen was perfectly fluent in French.

Ellen Grant Dalton's picture below was probably taken by Neil Bryan during his visit in 1952, she was 67 then.

Ellen Grant Dalton, photographed c. 1952 (courtesy of Sunraysia Daily, Mildura).

In 1953, Neil met Ellen again when he was living in Canada with his young wife. We know from archives that Ellen travelled by ship a few years later to Australia, she obviously liked travelling. We do not know, if she met Ken's parents on that occasion.

The Birdsalls returned to Washington DC in 1948. Paul joined the CIA in 1949 and was appointed later successively in Paris and Stockholm. Genevieve, on her side went back to the USA too where she married a journalist covering facts of war in the world, Mr Gordenker. She was living in New York. She divorced a few years later and came back to France in 1951, living in Neuilly and La Villeneuve.

I went for the first time with her in 1953 to the Le Bourget Air show, she was working for Loreal at the time and was the first to speak to me about the Dassault family, speaking of Marcel in elogious terms. It was the epoch of jet fighters Ouragan and Mystere IV, mythic planes of my chilhood as well as famous test pilots Constantin Rozanoff and Jacqueline Auriol.

Constantin "Kostia" Rozanoff, born in Poland, had graduated from Ecole Centrale and SupAero in 1933, a schoolmate of Marcel Dassault (graduated twenty years before in 1913), a College that I graduated from in 1967. He was killed during a flight demonstration in 1954 in Melun Villaroche flying a "Mystere IV", a plane with which he had been the first to fly above Mach 1 (the sound barrier) in France.

"Pussy" - Anne-Marie Sanderson – spent one year at home in 1952/53. My parents retired in Poiroux, Vendée in 1957, a province where my father had all his family roots. They were quite close to the Cherbonniers when they were in the Chevreuse valley, I don't think they met them or Anne-Marie after they retired in Vendée.

The surprising thing with this story is that my parents never met the Rivieres, Ellen Grant Dalton and other members of the crew when they came back to La Celle-les-Bordes, with the exception of Colin Guy in 1946 and maybe William D. Guy in June 1953, another cousin of F/S R. C. Guy, living in Ottawa. He was at the time a medical student in Mc Guill University, Montreal.

He was searching for the place where the Lancaster had crashed in 1944 with a friend. Somebody, - a Citroen car passing through, drove them to the Memorial and indicated the location of the Cemetery nearby. It could very well have been my father who had a Citroen car and there were not that many cars in the county at that time. They did not find the tail wreckage which was still there, 1500 yards behind the Memorial in the forest.

The Sixties and Afterwards

Paul Birdsall belonged to the OSS during the war (source US archives). Thus he had been involved, with no doubt, in the "Carpetbagger" operation when he was in London. He retired from CIA in 1962 and went to the Virgin Islands, in Christiansted. It is an independent US territory, to the East of Porto Rico.

I found in US archives some press articles about Marthe, in the Daily Messenger, Canandaigua, a city in the North East of New York state, where she went from time to time and where they probably had a family property.

My father passed away, in January 1966, a few days before Maurice Cherbonnier. A Ceremony was organised in Chevreuse on November 11th, 1966 to pay a special tribute to Maurice, for what he did during the war.

On this occasion, Ken Chapman, who had kept solid links with the family, especially Janine, came from England and made a speech when a plaque was unveiled on the wall of their house. Ken, as we know, was fluent in French.

Ellen Grant Dalton was then residing in Brighton and Belgium. She passed away in London in May 1968, she was about 83. The Funeral was held in Lyndhurst, where she was buried and where she had her roots, certainly the place where Ken had spent a few week ends during the war.

Paul Birdsall passed away on May 2nd, 1970 in Christiansted, he was buried at sea on May 5th, 1970 a special ceremony authorised in the Virgin Islands. Paul was seventy years old. Marthe, who was so nice to me, passed away a few yers later in Christiansted too, in January 1974.

Genevieve was living at that time in Chambourcy, near Plaisir. The last time I spoke to her on the phone was in May 1975. She was about to go back living in the USA, I was about to be transferred to West Africa and I lost track of her.

Jo in her research, found a poignant letter hand written by Anne-Marie when General de Gaulle died in 1970 (see Appendix 8) mailed to Mr. & Mrs. G Baillon, the pork butcher delivering food to airmen through Comet Line during the war. A copy of the letter was given to Jo by Denise Baillon, their daughter who remembers Anne-Marie very well, an "impressive beautiful woman". Denise, born in the thirties, delivered food to airmen from time to time.

The letter begins with "My name was Antoinette in those times.." It clearly expresses her strong desire to fight the Nazis beside General de Gaulle and the feelings she had thirty year later with his "unbearable" death.

We know now better what Anne-Marie did during the war risking her own life, without any doubt with all the testimonies we have gathered. It seems to me now that she has not been properly rewarded for what she did and the number of lives she saved. Probably, like many others who did the same, she did not care too much about honors. They were not the reason why she did what she did.

I recently learnt – following a private donation – that the American Historical Association (AHA) had decided in the eighties to grant every two years a prize "Paul M Birdsall" to an American or Canadian Historian having published a document about the Strategy of USA in Europe or in the World.

Another amazing story. Hans Gatzke, the donor, was German and met Paul in Williams College in 1938, where Paul was the Dean. Instead of coming back to Germany when war started, Hans stayed in USA and joined the OSS with Paul. They surely were working together in London, where Hans' knowledge of Germany was surely highly appreciated, and were both certainly involved in the Carpetbagger operation.

Hans Gatzke made his anonymous donation in 1985, fifteen years after Paul's death to finance the prize "Paul M Birdsall". His name has only been revealed after his death. He was probably fearing retaliation measures against his family in Germany.

The Removal of DS822's Engines from the Forest

I made the assumption the nose of the Lancaster could hardly fly more than one minute after plane broke up, spinning out of control, without her tail, with two engines pulling her to the left.

We know (from J. L. Riviere) that a fire had developed on the Clairefontaine side of the forest, north of the D27. The explosion which occurred when she crashed, from the 750 gallons of gasoline left on board, certainly threw metallic parts within a circle of about half a mile's radius.

After having pursued investigations with surrounding counties, including La Celle-les-Bordes plateau in the north of the D61, I did not find anything. I ended up with the conclusion that the plane crashed most probably in the forest, without making any other damage than those brought to trees, rabbits, pheasants and deer. Unfortunately, Waters & Forest archives – which normally would have had some forest guards' statements - were not available for that period.

I gathered several other testimonies of interest.

•   Henri Kergreis who was hunting in the area in the Seventies, remembered having seen many metallic parts in the sector North of D27 going from Rambouillet to Clairefontaine.

•   Jean Huon remembered that a large thick steel plate had been found in Clairefontaine. It could be the Lancaster armoured steel plate protecting the pilot behind his seat. We also checked that only one large bomber of Lancaster size had crashed in the area.

•   Bernard Cherrie a former Boeing 747 captain, living in St. Remy, had also been hunting in the area. He remembered that very large engines had been taken out in 1975, in an area close to D27 and D61.

•   We found the policeman Michel Leblanc, who witnessed the removal of these engines in the seventies, in a place close - from what he says – to Parc de la Verrerie. Unfortunately we did not find any trace in the

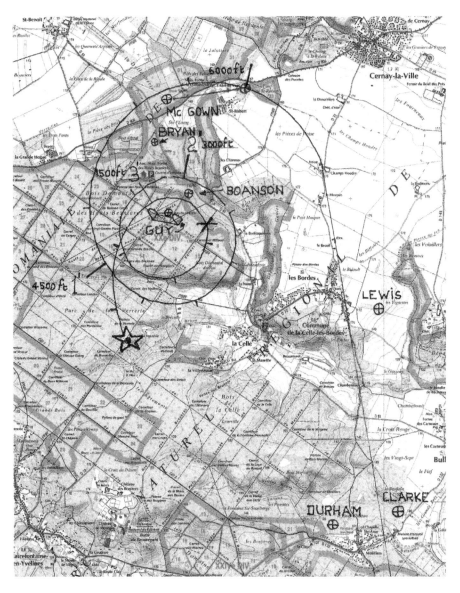

The locations of landing for the surviving crew members from DS822, and the crash site of the Lancaster herself (star).

FAF or Air Police archives, the engines having probably been transported to Evreux or Villacoublay air force bases and destroyed since.

• Michel Leblanc remembers also a two machine guns which were found in good condition, deeply sunk in the mud, which protected the turret from corrosion. It was most probably the forward (or mid-upper) turret of the Lancaster.

A part of a gun turret with a piece of Perspex riveted to the frame (author's photo).

Here is where we stand to day. All findings converge towards an area which should be around the Parc of La Verrerie. All heavy or large parts, wings, fuselage, engines, and so on were probably recovered in the Seventies, like the tail but we are sure that hundreds of metallic parts scattered in the explosion are still there in the forest.

The Germans forbade anyone from touching anything falling from the sky. So the area of the crash and wreck would certainly have been closely watched for a while, to allow the Germans to take back all interesting parts like radio transmitters, navigation aids, radars. In 1944, villagers could certainly not approach the site of the wreck, which explains why not many testimonies were found, like those we had for the tail which was only looked for one morning.

By comparison with other sites, many metallic aluminum parts are still there in the forest, as well as unexploded ammunition. Hunters, mushrooms seekers, walkers, will continue to find them from time to time, with or without a metal detector. The best periods for searching for parts are those when grasses are gone, in early March or November. The only precautions to take are linked to unexploded ammunition, they may be unstable and dangerous if disturbed.

So we will stop our research here, leaving some mystery and unanswered questions to the story. We are not too anxious about the conclusions. The plane crashed for sure in the area identified, the engines removed surely came from DS822.

Obviously, it would be better to find in the RAF or the Waters & Forests archives more detailed information on where the crash occured and a record of the engines' serial numbers. This information might well be stored somewhere, just like hundreds of aluminum parts left in the forest.

Meetings of the 'Lancaster Family'

Year after year, we have built up a solid group of contributors that we call now the 'Lancaster Family'. Our meetings are organised often spontaneously, with short notice, taking advantage of everybody's travel plans.

Meetings are always warm and bring the same sympathy from contributors to research and a few others interested in past history. We have summarised here below the key events which occured, year after year.

2009

Deer hunting in La Celle-les-Bordes anthology gave me a unique opportunity in May 2009 to gather with the help of Mayor Serge Querard former classmates of the Primary school in the forties and collect on the same occasion some testimonies about the crash of our Lancaster in 1944.
An efficient meeting and moving reunion; some shed a tear when they were seated on the benches of their old school.

Right after, we met R.C. Guy's cousins - Jean and Sinclair Ronald - with Ydoine Riviere, the Clairefontaine Angel who buried Bertie in the forest in June 1944. We went to the place where the tail with their cousin fell in the woods. The tail of the Lancaster has been removed from the forest, we can't approach the site anymore, new trees have been planted and the area is closed with a fence for tree regeneration. When we were approaching the place on a forest track, a deer crossed the track just in front of us. It was not unusual as there are many of them in the forest, but maybe it was a sign of destiny.

My first visit to Waterbeach was also a unique moment with a Lancaster fly past above the main 04/22 runway. I almost felt I was in the plane when she was making sharp turns to come back. I remember sad feelings everybody had when we saw her disappearing on the horizon. During the service in St John's, the reverend thanked my parents for what they had done during the war and my research on DS822.

We were then able to contact John Tanney, thanks to Sinclair Ronald. John had recorded his own story and immediately involved himself in our research. For Christmas he bought a computer to be able to communicate with us on the internet. On several occasions, he helped me with Lancaster technical problems, identification of parts found in the forest, procedures used to bale out, and circumstances about his accident when he came back from Nuremberg. Soon after, Lisa Ydoine Todd announced that she would come to visit us from Melbourne with her husband Alex.

2010

When Lisa Ydoine and Alex Todd confirmed their visit in May Yvonne and Marc Darbonne offered spontaneously their help for the organisation of the visit. Marc is a great friend of our family, probably with Yvonne the oldest persons knowing me since I was born. They must be about the same age as Genevieve Proix. Marc had my father as a teacher when he was in primary school in Milly la Foret, before La Celle-les-Bordes.

More than that, Marc met for the first time his wife Yvonne Roy in La Celle-les-Bordes. She was the daughter of one of my father's best friend, an artist Emile Roy living in Les Sables d'Olonne (Vendée). In 1940, the Germans occupied France and expelled populations living near the sea shore, forcing them to relocate at a distance of about ten miles and preventing them from sending signals to ships at sea.

This is the reason why at this time, my parents lent their house to Yvonne parents in Poiroux. It was at the right distance from the sea shore for the Germans. Yvonne at the time was studying Fine Arts in Nantes and she was going there in company of another student living in Poiroux, Aymard de Lezardiere.

In July 1945, Marc was invited one Sunday with his parents for lunch at home. It happened that Yvonne was also there at home that very day. As our dining room was too small for the number of guests, my mother utilised the council meeting room to receive her guests, which was on the same floor.

Marc and Yvonne were seated side by side during the lunch, under the "Marianne[30]" of the time. The next day, Marc called my mother asking what he could do to meet again Yvonne. My mother - a straight talker - said

---

[30] 'Marianne' is the bust of a beautiful woman personifying the Republic that you find in France in every Town Hall meeting room for wedding ceremonies.

Lisa Todd, F Ydier, Alex Todd, Ydoine Riviere, Solange Marchal and Serge Querard (author's photo).

to Marc, "Pay attention, Yvonne is a serious girl, you won't see her again if it is just to fool around."

Marc answered, "I don't want to play around, I just want to marry her." It was love at first sight and destiny had organised their meeting.

My father had identified Marc as a gifted man when he was in primary school. He became later the world's leading expert for the culture of medical plants. Yvonne certainly contributed to his successes so, as the proverb says, "Cherchez la femme (Find the lady)."

When Lisa arrived in Paris, Marc invited us all in company of Ydoine Riviere near Place de l'Etoile. The next day, we all met in La Celle-les-Bordes near the church and Chateau. All our friends were there, husband and wives Mayor Querard, MM Blanluet, Darbonne, Devilliers, Guernon, Huon, Poisson, Populaire and Ydier. Solange Marchal honoured us with her

179

presence during the visit, in company of her daughter Isabelle de Lezardiere, having that day another family commitment.

It was a great pilgrimage, in many respects. We went to the Memorial in the forest where poppies placed in November were still there, to the cemetery where Lisa Ydoine brought flowers on her uncle's grave, and then the old "Mairie-Ecole" reopened by Mayor Querard for the occasion, where Marc and Yvonne had met for the first time. We went then to the new Town Hall, where Serge offered to guests, the "verre de l'amitie", a friendship cocktail.

Yvonne, when entering the cocktail room, immediately recognised "her" old Marianne who had been kept in the transfer to the Town Hall new building, the one under whom she had met her husband for the first time sixty five year before. A totally unforeseen meeting, chance had organised - one more time – the meeting went quite well.

Marc made a short speech, quite emotional, then Mayor Serge Querard welcomed all the guests of the "Lancaster family". I was translating live in English or French. When Lisa Ydoine started speaking after Mayor Querard, she said upfront. I am going to answer the nice words that you said to my attention, I wish to warn you in advance, I am sure I am going to cry.

At the end, everybody was shedding a tear, including Alex and I who were supposed to be translating.

The same thing had happened two years before, when we had established at night a video conference connection between La Celle-les-Bordes with Mildura and Melbourne.

Another beautiful day, to be paying a tribute to the "boys" with the presence of the Lancaster family, honouring the visit of Kenneth Bryan's niece, Lisa Ydoine and celebrating the 65th anniversary of the first Marc and Yvonne meeting in La Celle-les-Bordes.

We had a nice lunch all together in Rambouillet. Then, the most courageous went walking in the forest near the place where we thought the Lancaster had ended up her flight. Unfortunately, we did not find any metallic part coming from the plane as the grasses were too high.

180

The 65th anniversary of their first meeting, May 2010. Marc and Yvonne under the protection of Marianne (courtesy of Jacques Blanuet).

Jean Ronald (R. C. Guy's cousin), John Tanney (replaced by R. C. Guy in the crew) and Lisa Ydoine Todd (niece of K. E. Bryan) at the Memorial Garden on Waterbeach airfield (courtesy of Sinclair Ronald).

During the walk, Lisa Ydoine told me that her father Neil was following day by day meetings she had in Europe. Then we came back in Paul and Martine Poisson's home who offered a drink to the brave walkers and we ended the visit in Choisel Town Hall where Roger Guernon had displayed panels developed for the 2009 exhibit.

The next day Lisa and Alex flew away to London, and the following Wednesday had a meeting with the Ronald's in Waterbeach. The above historical picture summarises and represents a part of the crew as it was 66 years before. It shows Jean Ronald (Guy), John Tanney and Lisa Todd (Bryan) surrounding the Memorial unveiled in June 2009 by the Commanding Officer of Waterbeach Barracks, Colonel Stove.

John Tanney drove down from the North of England with his son Paul to meet Alex and Lisa Ydoine, the niece of his former room mate in Waterbeach, Kenneth Bryan with whom he had at least twelve combat operations (see Appendix 5). That day, Paul Tanney said to Sinclair Ronald,

"I have learnt more in two hours about what my father did during the war than during the previous fifty years." People did not speak much in those days, as I said before.

Ariane Riviere, Ydoine's grand daughter, born in Sao Paulo made a long trip to Australia in 2009. Soon before her return, in June 2010, she made a pilgrimage to Mildura, hosted by Valda and Kenneth Wright in their home. She visited the Mildura RSL RAAF Museum with Kenneth and found the picture of her grand mother first called the "Angel of Clairefontaine" by Kenneth, displayed prominently in the Ken Bryan exhibit.

It was another great meeting of the "Lancaster family", in the native city of Ken Bryan, who had been buried in Rambouillet forest by her grand parents, Jean Louis and Ydoine Riviere, on June 10th, 1944. Ariane's visit to the Museum, has of course been honoured by the local press, "Mildura Weekly" which published the nice article below.

Courtesy of Alan Erskine, Mildura Weekly.

In the District of Mildura, 83 Australians served in the RAF Bomber Command during the war. 25 did not come back, 5 were held prisoners. Ken Bryan was the only one from 514 Squadron.

A Memorial in Mildura pays a tribute to the Memory of all those brave men, as does the Memorial in the Rambouillet forest, built and financed by Ellen Grant Dalton in 1950. Ellen Grant Dalton's picture taken from a Sunraysia daily press article, was probably taken by Neil Bryan in 1952, during his visit in France. Ellen was at the time 67, she met Neil Bryan in Canada in 1953 and probably Ken Bryan's parents in 1960 in Australia.

2011

The family of Lyndon Lewis

We had difficulty in tracing Lyndon Lewis's family archives, because he had been working for MI5 / MI6 after the war and he had disappeared from files. Roger Guernon and Sinclair Ronalds' research was eventually successful and Sinclair managed to establish contact in England with Clive Lewis.

In May 2011, Clive Lewis and his sister Geraldine Furk visited us and La Celle-les-Bordes. Another moving visit, in company of Ydoine Riviere and the other friends of the Lancaster family. They were lucky also, as a part of Choisel exhibit had been taken back for a few weeks by Chevreuse Town Hall and panels telling the story of DS822 were displayed in an old Tannery.

Clive and Geraldine were surprised when they visited the exhibit in Chevreuse to discover a number of pictures showing their father on the walls. They were also greatly appreciative of the dedication that must have gone into preparing the exhibition and of the respect shown to the Airmen who flew and gave their lives, in their fight for freedom.

Countess Andree de Jongh

In researching the Countess of Montenegro my mother was referring to when she was speaking about the escape of aviators through Basque country, I was misled by Andrée de Jongh story, who was at the head of Comet Line and became a Countess in 1986. I was speaking around about her story which is quite exceptional, when I discovered that from the terrace of the house I bought in 1998, I could see the place where Andree de Jongh was arrested in 1943, another unexpected coïncidence .

In addition I found another witness of her arrest. Elisabeth Mendiburu. She saw Andrée de Jongh, the farmer Frantzia Usandisaga her valet Juan Larburu and three airmen William Greaves, George Ross and Stanley Hope all hands on their heads with German soldiers in arms behind, at the bus stop in Urrugne leaving for Bayonne.

Seated: Elisabeth Mendiburu, her son "Pampi", Standing: Perrine Saveri, François Ydier and Jean Ronald (courtesy of Sinclair Ronald).

Elisabeth is the mother in law of Perrine Saveri who helps Françoise at home when we have our grand children. When I told the story to the Ronalds, they flew right away to the Basque country and we all met together Elisabeth and her family. She was 17 in January 1943, living on a farm close to Frantzia's one, "Bideguainberri". We had the luck to meet again Elisabeth, just before she passed away on January 19th, 2013 almost 70 years after the arrest, a sad anniversary.

Andrée, Frantzia (leaving behind her three children), and Juan were transferred to the Bordeaux and Fresnes prisons. Andrée and Frantzia were deported to Ravensbruck. Juan was deported to Dora camp, an annex of

Buchenwald camp, 45 miles in the South. Juan – being Spanish - was hoping he would be freed quickly, but he died there on February 22nd, 1944.

I wish also to pay a tribute to the Dassie family. Jean, Marthe and Lucienne who was only 16 at the time. They had sheltered the day before Andrée and two airmen in Bayonne. They were identified in March 1943 when the Gestapo asked airmen to show them the streets they had been through.

The Dassie family was also jailed in Fresnes, Jean had been deported to Buchenwald, Marthe and her daughter Lucienne were deported to Ravensbruck. Lucienne is one of those who said, "If I had to do it all again, I would."

Lucienne Dassie (Saboulard) is still alive, I hope I have the chance to meet her one day in the Basque country. Every year in September the Comet Line organises meetings there with veterans of the tragedy they had been through during the war.

Neil and Lisa Bryan

In October Jean and Sinclair Ronald made a trip to Australia, New Zealand and the Fiji Islands. On that occasion they met Neil Bryan and his daughter Lisa Ydoine in Melbourne. Whilst travelling in New Zealand they visited the place where Phillip Lamason had previously been living but no one knew his forwarding address, so unfortunately they could not see him.

Elvire de Brissac

We were just missing Elvire in our meetings. She did not want to go back to La Celle-les-Bordes, as the Chateau had been sold since her childhood, and I understood her reasons. So we went to visit her, in company of Martine and Paul Poisson, born, like me, in 1942.

A great meeting on November 6th, 2011 very emotional, the past was coming back as if it was yesterday. We did not have to speak, history was there, and we got together in Apremont sur Allier like old accomplices, as if time had stopped for sixty years.

Elvire is a writer of romances, several of her books having been awarded literature prizes. She is another great lady from La Celle-les-Bordes. Without knowing it, we were in good company in the village. The place is simply magic.

Alex & Lisa Ydoine Todd, Neil Bryan, Jean Ronald (courtesy of Sinclair Ronald).

From L to R. Martine, Paul, Elvire and François

Apremont sur Allier – chateau and floral park (courtesy of Elvire de Brissac).

Elvire now lives in one of the most beautiful villages in France, Apremont Sur Allier. Her brother Gilles developed there a magnificent floral park. Elvire continues to maintain it with a master hand, as well as a very nice 15th century castle alongside which belonged to their mother.

2012

A great year for the Lancaster family, with discoveries beyond our greatest expectations.

January: I found again, by chance, my childhood friend Anne-Marie Sanderson and Geraldine Cerf de Dudzeele, the daughter of Countess of Montenegro, I had been searching for the last five years. I met her with Josselyne Lejeune Pichon who had been working on her side for quite a few years and had found the trace of Anne-Maries' grand parents, which was a decisive finding which helped me to find "Pussy", or Anne-Marie, then Géraldine the Countess of Montenegro's daughter.

March: Thanks to Serge Querard and Thierry Boche, research on P47 shot down above La Celle-les-Bordes in 1944 made fantastic progress as we saw when we started to communicate with Paul Stouffer, Robert

Carmody and Bill Sheppard. Paul sent me a few days later the picture of Buttner's P47 shot down in La Villeneuve on August 15th, 1944 . The plane had been before Gabby Gabresky's, one of the USAAF greatest heroes during WW II.

    May: Gillian Dean, John Clarke's daughter, decided to have a trip around the world, visiting Nepal, Australia and New Zealand. After having found the trace of Anne-Marie Sanderson, I realised that John Clarke had been sheltered by the Kalmansons in 1944 in the same house, one month before, as Phillip Lamason and Ken Chapman. Anne-Marie Sanderson's family had kept strong links with Ken Chapman, throughout their lives. On the other hand, Roger Guernon had been in contact with Christie Lamason for the Choisel exhibition. It seemed obvious then, they had a unique opportunity to meet each other in Australia or New Zealand.

Gillian Dean and Christie Lamason, May 13th 2013 Auckland (courtesy of Gillian Dean).

We knew that Phillip Lamason saved the life of 168 aviators when he was in Buchenwald with John Clarke and Ken Chapman, and without Phillip, none of them would have survived. On May 13th, Christie met Gillian in Auckland, as picture shows.

The next day, Monday May 14th, John Tanney passed away peacefully, at the age of 90. He had been following our research up to the end. On Saturday May 19th, Phillip Lamason passed away at the age of 93. Christie had warned us before, she was not sure that Phillip would survive another cold winter in New Zealand. The month of May has always been an important month for our meetings and events related to the Lancaster family.

The Lancaster Family at the 514 Squadron Renuion, Waterbeach, June 16th 2012. Family links to crew members are mentioned in brackets.

Front Row: Ian Kershaw - Stan Kershaw - Beryl Kershaw (G Boanson) - Francois Ydier – HRH Daisy Clarke (J Clarke) - Francoise Ydier - Jean Ronald (R Guy). Second Row: Carl Lewis (G Boanson - Stan Kershaw grandson) - Russell Kershaw (G Boanson) – Sinclair Ronald (R Guy) - Gillian Dean - Rachel Clarke (J Clarke) – Geraldine Furk – Rosemary Lewis - Marilyn Hocking (L Lewis) Back Row: Clive Lewis - Ray Hocking (L Lewis) (Courtesy of Stan Kershaw).

St John's Church, Waterbeach, for the annual memorial service for 514 Squadron, June 16th 2012. Leslie Sutton, DFC with his grand children (courtesy of Stan Kershaw).

The annual reunion of 514 Squadron veterans and their families was held on June 16th, 2012. It was the final time it was held on the site as a military base. Waterbeach Barracks, formerly RAF Station Waterbeach, closed in March 2013 after 72 years. However, agreement has been reached with the site's new owners to maintain the Waterneach Military Heritage Museum at the entrance and 2015 saw the reunion held there after two years 'in exile' in the village hall.

The picture (previous page) of the "Lancaster family" was taken in front of the entrance to the Mess to commemorate such a great moment. The memory of Johhn Tanney was saluted during the service conducted in St John's Church by the Reverend Pamela Thorn. The Fly Past which was supposed to be held right after was cancelled because of bad weather conditions.

I heard some Veterans saying. "They were paying less attention to winds when we were leaving for Ops!" Over lunch, I had the opportunity to speak with Leslie Sutton, copilot of the second 514 Squadron Lancaster shot down the same night, LL727. A book, "Skid Row to Buckingham Palace" has just been published[31]. It tells the story of the plane and her skipper F/O. Louis Greenburgh DFC.

It was quite a surprise when Leslie, seeing my book and Anne-Marie de Dudzeeles' picture said. "I know this lady." It transpired that Louis Greenburgh escaped from LL727, was rescued by members of the "Comet Line" and stayed in the airmens' camp in Freteval Forest until they were liberated by advancing allied troops.

I said before, the story fell into my lap. I could not imagine I would find so many coïncidences and so many people having a link with the story that destiny placed on my road:

- Géraldine Cerf de Dudzeele, Anne-Marie de Dudzeele's daughter,
- Francis Gabreski former Razorback P 47 pilot
- William Sheppard shot down in La Villeneuve in August 1944,
- Leslie Sutton, a great witness of the June 8th fateful night,
- Christiane Leteissier, from Poigny la Foret who had the visit of Pop Seddon's family,
- Suzanne Siffroi (Daifeli) who lived for twenty years in Moulin des Clayes,
- Ngaire Nystrup, who knew Phillip Lamason for fifty years.

It was meant to be.

In my research about the Proix and Birdsall families, I also discovered in 2012 that a prize was given to an American or Canadian historian every two years by Association "AAH". The year 2012 was certainly a great year to end up the research and decide to publish the story.

---

[31] 'Skid Row to Buckingham Palace' is the autobiography of F/L Lou Greenburgh, DFC and Bar, as told to his son Ed Greenburgh. Published 2016 by Mention the War Ltd.

The Bomber Command Memorial, Green Park, London

HM Queen Elizabeth II opens the Bomber Command Memorial on June 28th 2012.

On June 28th, 2012 an impressive Memorial dedicated to RAF Bomber Command aircrew was unveiled by the Queen in company of the Royal Family in Green Park in London, the year of her Diamond Jubilee. Could we also imagine a more prestigious end to our story, written in golden letters?

Many veterans came from all over the world to salute the event. This celebration put an end to sixty years of controversy about the role played by the RAF Strategic Bombing during the war under the firm direction of "Bomber Harris", as Churchill used to call him. A Lancaster flew over during ceremony to salute the Queen and Memorial. She dropped poppies to the great surprise of children playing in Green Park.

We only regret that Ellen Grant Dalton is not with us anymore. Her family on both sides, Gant and Grant Dalton, had been living for a long time

HM Queen Elizabeth II, HRH the Duke of Edinburgh, HRH the Prince of Wales and Camilla, Duchess of Cornwall paid a fitting tribute to the heroes of Bomber Command at the opening of the memorial in Green Park, London.

in this beautiful neighbourhood of London and she would certainly have been a guest of honor, having done what she had done sixty years before.

I am sure she would have thought, "I have done the same some years ago".

George, Ken, Robert and all of the other "boys" of Bomber Command, we are still with you. We will never forget you.

William McGown can now rest in peace with his decorations, justice has been done at last.

The Boy and the Bomber

Avro Lancaster PA474 of the Battle of Britain Memorial Flight (above)dropped poppies to commemorate the 55,573 aircrew lost whilst serving with Bomber Command in the war. The bomber and the poppies delighted many young children playing in the park (below).

Last Meetings, Events and Witnesses

On October 25th, I had the pleasure to meet Ngaire Nystrup from New Zealand, living in Denmark when she was visiting Paris. She personally knew for years Phillip Lamasons' family. She had dinner with Denise Kalmanson and her nephew, Antoine Poliet, Colette's son. Ngaire confirmed that Phillip was a very humble man, hardly speaking about war, although he spoke a little more after his wife passed away. She thinks proper recognition has not been given to him in New Zealand for what he did during war, before the film telling the story of his deportation to Buchenwald was released. Her brother Hoani Hansen (also a name of Maori origin) had worked in Phillip's Rua Roa Farm, in Dannevirke.

It should probably be fair and a great idea, to keep alive Phillip's memory in his home country, to give his name to an airport there. We leave, of course such a suggestion, to the appropriate authorities.

OTHER WITNESSES

On December 8th 2012 we met with Geraldine Cerf de Dudzeele two 1944 key witnesses of our story.

Suzanne Siffroi (Daifeli)

Suzanne was born in 1929, the daughter of the cook working for the Douglas and de Dudzeele families. Suzanne lived for about twenty years in the Moulin, from from 1935 until 1957. She confirms German officers lived in the house which had been requisitioned in 1941. Her room was between the Germans ones on the first floor and Edward Douglas's Sculptor studio. She knew Anne-Marie quite well as a teenager, and confirms she totally ignored what she was going on in the Underground. Her first words when she saw Geraldine sixty five year later were "You look like your mother".

Her childhood friend, Roger Boschet, whose father was keeping the wine store in St. Remy, said the same thing. He remembers very well Anne-Marie and was surprised by the quantity of alcohol he was delivering to the house, obviously for the use of the airmen. Alcoholic spirits were rare during the war.

The Boy and the Bomber

Above: Ngaire Nystrup and Denise Lamason on October 25th 2012 (courtesy of Antoine Poliet). Below: Hoani Hansen and Phillip Lamason in 2008, Rua Roa Farm, N.Z. (courtesy of Ngaire Nystrup).

Nicolas Ruelle Géraldine Cerf de Dudzeele, and Suzanne Siffroiin at "Moulin des Clayes" (courtesy of Geraldine Cerf de Dudzeele)

Christiane Letessier

Christiane was brought up by her grandmother, Mrs. Angélique Bie, after her mother had passed away at a very young age. She brought her memories as well as those of her grand mother, they have already been included in our story.

The Hotel Restaurant "Le Petit Paris" was managed by her grandmother. Located at the corner of two roads, D108 and D936, in the country, it was a convenient place to organise discrete meetings with aviators, without attracting attention.

Bill Leihsmann remembers that the Germans were only a few yards away from the group of airmen and Resistance members, a truly frightening thought.

When she was visiting the Hotel, Anne-Marie was about 15 miles from home, we understand very well now why she was sleeping in the Hotel

Elio Zannier, Christiane Letessier and Geraldine Cerf de Dudzeele in Poigny-la-Foret (courtesy of Geraldine Cerf de Dudzeele).

from time to time. When it was late in the evening, cycling back in the dark and through the forest was certainly a stressing experience, even with a dog and a gun.

A former Mayor of Poigny la Foret, Elio Zannier, joined us during the visit. Christiane had also been an Assistant to the Mayor during three terms. They told us that in 1948, the boxer Marcel Cerdan, who was training in a sport centre nearby, stayed in the hotel with his mistress, the singer Edith Piaf. She was knitting while she waited for him.

The Last Flight of Kenneth Wright

On Sunday, 28th January 2013 Kenneth celebrated the 69th anniversary of his first solo flight in the RAAF in a Tiger Moth biplane. Kenneth, at the age of 87, has decided to stop piloting planes. To celebrate the event, he made his final flight as a pilot with one of the last Tiger Moths still flying in Australia.

Kenneth Wright upon his return after he flew the Tiger Moth VH-NWM (courtesy of Sunraysia Daily).

Kenneth told me he was a bit disappointed, because the Tiger Moth's owner would not allow him to fly under the bridge which spans over the Murray River in Mildura. Watching the pictures, I must confess the height of the bridge is not sufficient to fly under it with any degree of safety!

On May 8th, 2013 Neil Bryan passed away in Melbourne. May he now rest in peace with his dear wife Mamie. His letter "My brother Ken" (see Appendix 1) is displayed in the RAAF museum in Mildura. A minute of silence was observed there on May 17th, during a morning meeting in the Museum, to pay Neil a last tribute.

The Seventieth Anniversary

In 2014 many ceremonies were organised in France to mark the seventieth anniversary of D-Day. Our friends of the "Lancaster Family" made their own spontaneous contribution.

In September John and Debbie Lamason, Christie's parents and a friend Glenys Scott made a tour of Europe from New Zealand on the tracks of S/L. Phillip Lamason, the skipper of LM575 LS-H, MKIII Lancaster.

They arrived Sunday 14th night in Paris, went to Fresnes prison and of course met the Kalmanson family, Denise and her nephew Antoine Poliet, the son of Colette.

On September 16th, our visitors followed Phillip's escape in direction of Paris through Montfort L'Amaury where they spent a few days in the Cuillerier family house at Trappes, the location of the railway yards which had been Phillip's bombing target. They visited Chevreuse, where he was sheltered with his navigator Kenneth Chapman in Maurice Cherbonnier's book store and Kalmanson house and St. Remy Les Chevreuse where they took the train to Paris, escorted by Janine et Maurice Cherbonnier. The Belgian girl, "Antoinette" in the Comet Line had on several occasions met Phillip and Kenneth whilst organising their escape.

With of Roger Guernon and I, they went afterwards to Jouars Pontchartrain cemetery to take flowers and pay a tribute to W/O. R.B. Aiken RAF, 20 years old, the mid upper gunner of Phillip's crew, whose parachute opened too late to save him.

Then, together with Annick Lehman, we all went to Plaisir near by, to pay a tribute to F/O. T.W. Dunk, RAF, 30 years old, rear gunner of the plane who crashed with the tail of the Lancaster near Sainte Apolline woods.

After walking back from the cemetery to the Town Hall, Mrs. Mayor Joséphine Kollmannsberger and several deputies offered to us the "glass of friendship". Mrs. Mayor gave to John the City of Plaisir Book and a City medal engraved with the name of Phillip Lamason. John Lamason, in his answer to the Mayor gave her a letter from the Mayor of Dannevirke, where he lives in New Zealand. A quite emotional and beautiful friendly ceremony. At the end our guests sang their national anthem in Maori.

Above: W/O R.B. Aitken's grave in Jouars-Pontchartrain Cemetery. From L to R. Debbie Lamason – John Lamason – Annick Lehman deputy to the Mayor – Roger Guernon – Glenys Scott (courtesy of Annick Lehman). Below: F/O T.W. Dunk's grave in Plaisir Cemetery. From L to R. F. Ydier, P. Plantadis, J. Kollmannsberger, Mayor, Glenys Scott, J Lamason, and Debbie Lamason (courtesy of City of Plaisir).

On our way back to Paris, I had the surprise to receive a call from Mrs. Yolande Cuillerier. She was desappointed that her husband could not attend the ceremony in Plaisir because he remembers quite well Phillip Lamason who stayed several days in his parents' house in Montfort L'Amaury en 1944, he was 12 at the time.

We planned to organise another meeting with our visitors when they come back from Germany and Buchenwald.

On September 27th, Stan Kershaw, a cousin of J. G. S. Boanson came from England with his son and friend Carl Lewis to put on their graves the picture of the three DS822 airmen buried in La Celle-les-Bordes.

Stan took this opportunity to come back to the forest to the places where airmen's bodies had been found according to the 1944 legal book, close to the Memorial built in the fifties along road D 61 and the tail crash site.

On our way back to Plaisir we made a short stop over in front of the Solange Marchal "Château des Bordes" where Monique Dacheux was living next door. Lyndon Lewis had landed a few hundred yards on the left side and McGown was about to bale out when Monique saw the plane in flames in the dark.

Roger followed us, the weather was sunny and we had a friendly barbecue lunch at home. Our friends drove back safely on Monday from Rambouillet to England. We had just to wait for the "Three Musketeers" upon their return journey in Europe.

Eventually, Géraldine Cerf de Dudzeele invited everybody to a friendly dinner at home in Paris on Monday October 6th. Josselyne Lejeune Pichon (who traced Phillip's escape), Francis Cuillerier who remembers very well Phillip Lamason and Kenneth Chapman hidden with other airmen at home in Montfort L'Amaury, Françoise et Francois Ydier, and of course our three friends from New Zealand. It was a unique opportunity that we could not miss. Glenys Scott had composed a song to the tune of "*You are my sunshine*" to thank everybody. They all sang it in chorus, with Glenys playing her ukulele.

September 27th 2014. The photos of three RAF airmen, W/O. Ken Bryan, Sgt. J.G.S. Boanson, Sgt. R.C. Guy, displayed in front of their graves. From L to R. Colonel A Populaire, Mayor S. Querard, Stan Kershaw, F. Ydier, R. Guernon (courtesy of Stan Kershaw).

Josselyne Lejeune Pichon, Glenys Scott, Francis Cuillerier (author's photo)

Géraldine CERF de Dudzeele and Debbie Lamason (author's photo).

Our friends arrived back safely in New Zealand on Tuesday, October 7th. They were glad to come back to the "Green Green Grass" of their home after such a long journey. They have now just to catch up with the eleven hours time lag between Europe and New Zealand.

Two members of the Lancaster family left us in 2014. The first one was Hoani Hansen, Ngaire's brother, who passed away on October 29th, soon after the "Musketeers" came back to New Zealand from their European tour. He has left behind him by his dear wife and his three children. He is greatly missed.

With a great sadness we lost our dear 'HRH' Daisy Clarke on December 26th, 2014. Daisy had been a real ray of sunshine in our meetings, always happy to participate and making, like John Tanney, a magnificent contribution to our researches. God bless her and may she rests in peace, now that she has rejoined her husband John Clarke for Eternity.

More sad news arrived when we were about to end the story. Marc Darbonne passed away on April 1st, 2015 at the age of 94. He has left behind him his dear wife Yvonne and his four children Isabelle, Hubert, Luc and Hervé. Another exceptional character achieving his work on Earth, we will keep alive his memory. We present to his family our sincere condolences. God bless Marc, may he rest in peace now, before the Father and his Son.

Epilogue

It is the right time now to leave our dear Lancaster, though not without emotion. It was a long journey, it cannot be easy to leave the plane, the actors who made up her history and all members of the "Lancaster family" who helped in assembling the facts. What we have found on the way has only been friendship, adventure and richness which goes far beyond what an author could imagine.

In doing so, we were brought back to our childhood tracks, to La Celle-les-Bordes village history, to all aviators' families' history during the war. We went much further than the greatest expectancies we had when we began to write.

A great and beautiful story, sad however because it is a war story and there is no good in war.

When one sees the life of these brave, simple men, women and heroes who did not know they were heroes, you feel quite humble. Admiration comes first, before humility. We must remember their dedication, their unshakeable willingness to confront horrible situations, in spite of all the difficulties they were facing during their struggles.

We must be proud to keep the Memory of all these men and women who risked their lives to preserve our Freedom and build a better world.

Freedom like an eagle, was flying in their hearts.

My friend Elvire told me one day, "Your story will never end, it is my dearest wish."

Let's do the same, never forget them, as the poet said.

"They shall not grow old, as we are left grow old,
Age shall not weary them, nor the years condemn,
At the going of the Sun, and in the morning,
We will remember them."

Appendices

Appendix 1: My brother Ken   (Neil Bryan)
Appendix 2: Y. Riviere letter to Bryan Family
Appendix 3: DS822 Crew Choisel Panel Exhibit
Appendix 4: Kalmanson Aviators Certificate
Appendix 5: Crew combat missions (ops)
Appendix 6: 7 to 8 June 1944 Casualties
Appendix 7: Walter Borchers Victories – Luftwaffe
Appendix 8: Je M'Appelais (My Name Was) Antoinette
Appendix 9: Commonwealth War Grave Commission certificates J.G.S.
                Boanson / K.E. Bryan / R.C. Guy / C.M. Guy.
Appendix 10: Main Actors
Appendix 11: Deer hunting in LCLB and landing points in 1944.
Appendix 12: FAFL in 1940
Appendix 14: Abbreviations used

Two documents published in 2013/14 complement the story.

David Guy (OTTAWA) developed a video paying a tribute to his cousins
Robert and Charlie Guy.

http.//www.youtube.com/watch?feature=player_embedded&v=zuY2_5fsaBc

Three reference books detail the history and operations of 514 Squadron
during WWII. All are published by Mention the War Ltd. and available from
www.bombercommandbooks.com

"*Striking Through Clouds*" by Simon Hepworth & Andrew Porrelli.
"*Nothing Can Stop Us*" by Simon Hepworth & Andrew Porrelli with Harry
Dison.
"*Some of the Story of 514 Squadron – Lancasters at Waterbeach*" by Harry
Dison.

Appendix 1 Neil Bryan's Letter

The document is produced courtesy of Neil Bryan who tells, in a poignant story, how Ken Bryan passed away in 1944.

MY BROTHER KEN

I have decided to transcribe for posterity the events of my brother's tragic death which occured fifty years ago. To be exact it was June 7th 1944 when their plane was shot down. It was the day after D-day, the allied invasion of Europe to free the people from Nazi Domination.

Not that Ken's death deserved any more attention than the millions of young men who gave up their lives in that war, or for that matter all wars before and after. Our father had served in World War I he knew all about the horrors of war, so it was with reluctance he gave written permission for Ken to enlist.

Ken was the eldest in our family of three chidren, my sister enlisted in the A.W.A.S as well. Ken was seven years my senior, so I suppose I never knew him that well. My strongest memories are of a tall handsome young man with thick black eyebrows that knitted together. He worked in a bank, and had a rich baritone voice.

My brother enlisted in the Royal Australian Air Force. He was turned down as a pilot because of poor eyesight but was accepted for training as a wireless operator-gunner, referred to on their wings as a W.A.G. They were schooled at Maryborough in Queensland then after graduation were shipped directly to England where he was posted to an RAF Squadron of Lancaster Bombers. According to his log book, he flew many sorties.

It was common practice during the war time rest and recreational periods for many of the men to be billeted out to English families. Ken was fortunate to be sent to a woman by the name of Mrs. Grant-Dalton who had an exquisite cottage in the New Forest in Kent. She was a widow whose husband had served in the Royal Navy as a Rear-Admiral. She was a woman of wealth, and not without some influence. She lived very comfortably, having a housekeeper, a chauffeur driven Limousine and a flat on Sloane

Square in London. I mention her now because she plays a major role in the story.

On the night of June 7th, Ken's plane went on a sortie over Paris when they were hit by anti-aircraft fire. Four of the crew parachuted to safety while the remaining three were trapped in the aircraft as it plummeted to esrth in flames. It crashed in a forest about forty miles south-west of Paris. I have often thought about that event, and prayed my brother was already dead before the bomber went down.

At the moment the Lancaster crashed a young Frenchman by the name of Jean Louis Riviere was cycling through the forest of Rambouillet to his home in the village of Clairefontaine. He saw the plane come down in a ball of fire. Upon reaching his home he related the event to his wife Ydoine, the following morning the young couple cycled to the crash site where they discovered the three bodies from the wreckage. They took the dog-tags then proceeded to bury the remains alongside with what was left of the plane.

Just as they completed the burial, a car pulled up containing a German officer accompanied by two soldiers. The officers asked the Rivieres what they were doing whereupon receiving a satisfactory explanation he stepped forward to the graves, saluted, turned on his heel and departed without another word. He was described as an older man of the "old school".

My parents were notified firstly that Ken was missing in action, then later that he was dead.

Just before the war ended, a letter was received addressed to my mother. It was written entirely in French, signed by Ydoine Riviere. From the dog tags this young woman, who was in her early twenties, had obtained the names and addresses of the next of kin of the three men she and her husband had buried.

The letter was beyond my school-boy French so I took it to my high school French master to translate.

It was poignantly written with a full explanation of events. As the bodies were still in the forest, she requested permission to disinter the remains and rebury them in their own village churchyard with a formal burial service conducted by the village priest. It was also the desire to erect a monument at the crash site in commemoration of the first young men to die in their area during the liberation of France.

My mother replied granting permission. At the same time she arranged to have Madame Riviere's letter published in our local newspaper which subsequently drew a number of letters from other parents whose sons had been killed with no knowledge of their whereabouts. They all said the samething, that the letter gave them hope, that perhaps their sons have received a similar respect.

A copy of this letter was also sent by my mother to Mrs. Grant-Dalton. She replied saying how she was deeply touched by the actions of village of Clairefontaine, and as soon as travel into Europe was allowed she would go to visit the Rivieres.

A further letter from Mrs. Grant-Dalton told how she had visited the three graves now established in the churchyard. She went on to describe the resting place as one of great beauty, a low white brick wall surrounding the cemetery, the graves in a position where one could look out across the wallto the Rambouillet forest. She also explained how the villagers were very poorand had not been able to do anything about the monument, so she, Mrs. Grant-Dalton had commissioned an architect to design and build the monument at her expense.

In 1952 I had the pleasure of meeting Mrs. Grant-Dalton. I was on my way to Canada via England. I wrote to her telling her of my "impending trip". She wrote back to say she would be in Paris at the time of my arrival but for me to fly to France to meet her there.

I did as she suggested, we met in Paris airport and the next day we drove to Clairefontaine. First we went to the churchyard where I was pleased to see that not only had the war grave commission complied with my mother's wishes, but they had fitted official headstones complete with their names and the air-force insignis embossed on them. The graves were obviously well tended, a small bunch of flowers placed on each grave every week by the village. I turned and looked out over the low brick wall toward the forest which was now ablaze with autumn colours. My mother would have loved it. I cried, even though it all happened so many years ago.

When we drove into the forest to where the monument stood at the side of the road where Jean Louis witnessed the crash. It is quite beautiful, a solid granite stone standing about five feet tall with an arched window cut into it in relief, a cross fills the window with a Lancaster bomber banking across the sky behind the cross. Below the window the names of three men who were killed.

Before I left that spot I silently vowed that if ever I had a daughter somehow in her name I would use the name of Ydoine, the young woman who had shown such compassion.

It was not yet the end of the day. Mrs. Grant-Dalton has arranged to have afternoon tea with Monsieur Riviere the father of Jean Louis, the young couple had gone to live in Brazil. Mrs. Grant-Dalton translated our conversation, it was at this time that I found she had been in Paris and spoke the language like a native.

Many years later my wife and youngest daughter went again to Clairefontaine, while my eldest daughter completed the pilgrimage on her own.

Her name is Lisa Ydoine

Neil Bryan

Appendix 2 Ydoine Riviere letter sent in 1945

Pilot Officer Ken Bryan (410529) attended Mildura West and Mildura High Schools and, prior to enlistment in RAAF Aircrew on 30 January 1942, was a Bank Officer. After graduating as a Wireless Airgunner, he was posted to the UK and 514 Squadron RAF based at Waterbeach flying in Lancaster Heavy Bombers. His squadron was involved in "D Day " and sadly his aircraft was shot down over Rambouillet Forest in France. Villagers of La Celle found his body beside the aircraft wreckage and the entire village attended his funeral on 10 June 1944.

Donor - Neil Bryan (Brother)

Dear Sir,

Thanks to the R.A.A.F. I am now able to send you the snap shots that my husband and I took from your son's grave. By the way I feel I must write you all I know about his death.

The landing by the Allies had just begun, night and day the sky was full of allied planes. Thursday June 8th my husband came from Paris to meet me in a little village, Laifontaine in Rambouillette Forest, he told me he had seen the smoke of a plane in the woods.

The next day he went to see where exactly it was, and if we could do something useful - after having walked a long time we found it in the wood, in a lovely place on a little hill not far from a German plane which fell the same night, but of course nobody went to see that. There we saw some woodcutters and they told us that the plane crashed at 2.a.m. and had been watched over till now by the Germans and nobody was allowed to approach. As soon as the Germans had gone the woodcutters came and one had the chance to see the name of your son and he wrote it on a paper. Among the pieces of his plane he had found the body of your son, my husband and I were both heartbroken and once more angry against the Germans because they had left the plane without doing something for the body, and the woodcutters were afraid and didn't dare to do anything because they said a thing we already knew. It is not allowed by the Germans to touch anything falling from the sky. Of course it was not true, but however, we did not want to leave him like that and my husband and I decided to bury him. My husband began to make a cross but the woodcutters who were good people came to help us and they had tools to make a better cross. With my husband they dug a provisional grave near the plane. My husband wrote the name on the cross and I looked for some flowers.

In the evening we went to see the Cure for this village La Celle. The next day (Saturday) I went with my husband to the Cemetry in which the body had been placed the same morning by the Cure after what we told him.

There was yet a few flowers and we had brought a sheaf of flowers, blue, white and red, at this moment we took the snap shots 2 and 3. On Sunday the 10th the whole village and people of other villages walked in procession with the Cure to the Cemetry, their arms full of flowers of every kind. A few baby's had crowns of flowers and you can see them on the cross of 7 and 8 photos. On the right you can also notice the Lorraine Cross, on 4 you see the grave covered with the flowers, when everyone had passed in front of it we all sang "La Marseillaise" and "God Save The King", and then the people went away. I stayed with a few women and put the flowers in good order as you can see on 5 and 6 photos.

I want you to know that your son is not a stranger to us, we love him for what he did for us, for our liberation, we thank you for it and be sure we shall never forget it, and as long as he will stay in this lovely country of La Celle we shall look after him. He is our brother and there will always be some flowers on his grave.

I forgot to tell you that on Friday 9th when we were burying your son a German non-commissioned Officer came, and my husband went to tell him what we were doing - we gave him the name of your son and be saluted, he just came to note some numbers of some pieces of the plane - he did not say anything, when we had finished, or nearly, he saluted the grave before going away.

Before closing let me tell you dear Sir how proud you can be of your son, he had a big part in our liberation and for that I thank you with all my heart.

Best regards,

MADAME J.L. RIVIERE.

Appendix 3 Choisel Exhibit

Panel developed about DS822 for Choisel exhibit courtesy of Roger Guernon

Appendix 4 Chapman Lamason Clarke Certificate

Document testifies John Clarke (Ioher Clark), Phillip (Elll) Lamason and K.W. Chapman were sheltered by family Kalmanson in Chevreuse. Please note bad transcription of names which leaves no doubt of aviators passing through.

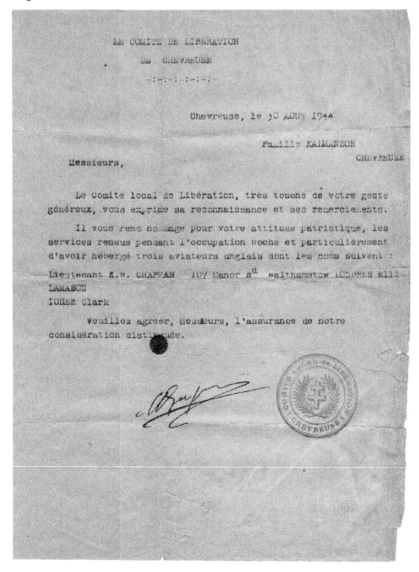

Appendix 5 DS822 Crew combat missions (ops)

APPENDIX 5   **CREW COMBAT MISSIONS 1943-1944**

DATE	PLANE		MISSION	HOURS		SKIPPER	NAV/G	BOMB AIM	RADIO	R GUN	M/GUN	ENGINEER	NOTES
03-nov-43	DS814	OPS	FRISIAN ISLANDS	2.3		MCGOWN	DURHAM	LEWIS	BRYAN	TANNEY	BOANSON	CLARKE	Mine laid at low rs
26-nov-43	DS 821	OPS	BERLIN	7.5		MCGOWN	RICKETTS	LEWIS	BRYAN	TANNEY	BOANSON	CLARKE	Sgt S V RICKETTS KILLED ON HIS 25th (LEIPZIG)
02-dec-43	DS822	OPS	BERLIN	7.2		MCGOWN	DURHAM	LEWIS	BRYAN	TANNEY	BOANSON	CLARKE	Damaged engined problem, missed unserviced
03-dec-43	DS 819	OPS	BERLIN	7.3	aborted	MCGOWN	DURHAM		BRYAN	TANNEY	BOANSON	CLARKE	
23-dec-43	DS816	OPS	BERLIN	7.3		ROBERTS	KILLOCK	RIPPINGALE	RICHARDSON	GUY	UDELL	COLES	Picked North Sea Dec 30th
29-dec-43	LL674	OPS	BERLIN	7.3		SYMONDS	BUTLER	BAMENT	STROMBERG	DRAKE	CAREY	WEDDLE	
27-jan-44	DS 821	OPS	LEIPZIG	7.3	aborted	GREENBURGH	DURHAM	LEWIS	BRYAN	SUTHERLAND	HENRY	CLARKE	
27-jan-44	LL574	OPS	BERLIN	7.4		MCGOWN	HALL	LEWIS		GUY			
28-jan-44	LL 668	OPS	BERLIN	7.3		MCGOWN	DURHAM	LEWIS	SUTHERLAND	HENRY	CLARKE		
15-feb-44	LL 603	OPS	LEIPZIG	7.3		MCGOWN	DURHAM	LEWIS	RICHARDSON	TANNEY	BOANSON	CLARKE	
19-feb-44	LL 655	OPS	STUTTGART	7.3		MCGOWN	DURHAM	LEWIS	BRYAN	TANNEY	BOANSON	CLARKE	
21-feb-44	LL 655	OPS	SCHWEINFURT	8		MCGOWN	DURHAM	LEWIS	BRYAN	TANNEY	BOANSON	CLARKE	
18-feb-44	LL 593	OPS	FRANKFURT	5.7		MCGOWN	DURHAM	LEWIS	BRYAN	TANNEY	BOANSON	CLARKE	
22-feb-44	LL 655	OPS	FRANKFURT	6.5		MCGOWN	DURHAM	SHEFERD	BRYAN	TANNEY	PATTISON	CLARKE	PATTISON AND SHEFERD KILLED IN LANDING
26-mar-44	LL 665	OPS	ESSEN	4.3		CHITTY	IVE	SHEFERD	FOX	GUY	PATTISON	PATTI	
22-mar-44	LL 616	OPS	FRANKFURT	7.3		MCGOWN	IVE		FOX	GUY	PATTISON	CLARKE	? DOANSON injured in CHORLEY (X3 IN LOG book)
30-mar-44	LU9U	OPS	NUREMBURG	9	collision	CHITTY	BAXTER	Mc CLENEGHAN	GILMORE	TANNEY	?	CLARKE	GUY text X4 3/4 crew here
18-apr-44	LL570	OPS	ROUEN	4.2		TORHAM	DURHAM	LEWIS	BRYAN	GUY	SCULLY	REID	
18-apr-44	DS 682	OPS	ROUEN	4.2		MCGOWN	DURHAM	LEWIS	BRYAN	BAHLE	BOANSON	CLARKE	
20-apr-44	DS 795	OPS	COLOGNE	4.6		MCGOWN	DURHAM	LEWIS	BRYAN	GUY	BOANSON	CLARKE	
24-apr-44	LL 594	OPS	DUSSELDORF	4.3		MCGOWN	DURHAM	LEWIS	BRYAN	GUY	BOANSON	CLARKE	
24-apr-44	DS 642	OPS	KARLSRUHE	6.6		MCGOWN	DURHAM	LEWIS	BRYAN	GUY	BOANSON	CLARKE	
27-apr-44	LL 620	OPS	FRIEDRICHSHAVEN	7.3		MCGOWN	DURHAM	LEWIS	BRYAN	GUY	BOANSON	CLARKE	
01-may-44	LL 620	OPS	CHAMBLY	3.6		MCGOWN	DURHAM	LEWIS	BRYAN	GUY	BOANSON	CLARKE	
06-may-44	LL 739	OPS	CAP GRIS NEZ	2		MCGOWN	DURHAM	LEWIS	BRYAN	GUY	BOANSON	CLARKE	
21-may-44	LL 620	OPS	DUISBURG	4.5		MCGOWN	DURHAM	LEWIS	BRYAN	GUY	BOANSON	CLARKE	
22-may-44	LL 625	OPS	DORTMUND	4.6		MCGOWN	DURHAM	LEWIS	BRYAN	GUY	BOANSON	CLARKE	
02-jun-44	LL 620	OPS	WISSANT	1.1		MCGOWN	DURHAM	LEWIS	BRYAN	GUY	BOANSON	CLARKE	
05-jun-44	LL 636	OPS	OURSTREHAM	3		MCGOWN	DURHAM	LEWIS	BRYAN	GUY	BOANSON	CLARKE	
08-jun-44	LL 620	US OPS	ST LO	1	Crash	MCGOWN	DURHAM	LEWIS	BRYAN	GUY	BOANSON	CLARKE	
08-jun-44	P47	OPS	M P VIIGG	2	Crash	GREENBURGH	R FOX	RIPPINGALE	STROMBERG	WOODNAM	CAREY	COLLINGWOOD	
09-jun-44	LL752	OPS	M P	2	Crash	LAMASON	CHAPMAN	MARPOLE	MUSGROVE	AITKEN	DUNK	GEORGE	
08-jun-44	LL 739	OPS	M P TRAPPES	1.7	Crain	HALL	IARVIS	SMITH	NORRIS	TILL	CUNRINGHAM	MAYHEAD	
09-jun-44	LM431	OPS	M P	1.6	Crash	SEDDON	LEISHMANN	HERD	DOVER	WOODWARD	TETLOW	WINDSOR	
09-jun-44	LK F?	OPS	VERSAILLES	1.5	Crain	MARINE	PERRIN	BONELL	STANNARD	WOODYID	PALMER	SMITH	
30-jun-44	LL 733	OPS	AMAYE / CAEN	1.2	no trace	CHITTY	DRIG		RICHARDSON	WELLS	JENNER	D.M BUY	
15-aug-44	P47	US OPS	LCLB	2	Crash	W J BUTTNER							
14 MK II	COMBAT		29 MISSIONS			25 MCGOWN	24 DURHAM	25 LEWIS	26 BRYAN	15 GUY	23 BOANSON	25 CLARKE	
25 X MK II							AUsF Files			Flying book	Flying book		
										12 TANNEY			

Appendix 6 Casualties of the Night of 7th/8th June 1944

ANNEXE 7
LOSSES JUNE 7/8th, 1944

ATTAQUES COMMUNICATIONS REGION PARISIENNE 7/8 JUIN 1944

OBJECTIF	USAAF	RAF	RCAF	RAAF	RNZAF	INJ	POW	EVD	KIA	UK	COMMENT	CRASH LOCATION
ACHERES 5		4	3						7		NO TRACE	?
		2	6				2	5	8		?	RONCHOIS SEINE MME
		1	8				2		1		CRASH	GALLON
		3	4				2	1	1		BACK UK	BENSON
			6								NF	GISORS (Pilot killed)
TOTAL ACHERES		11	25			0	6	10	17	3		
CHEVREUSE 6		4		3					2		NF	MASSY
		7					1	5	8		NF	MONTCHAUVET
		7							7		EXPLODED	GIVERNY
		6	1						7			PUTEAUX
		5	2						7		NF	BREVIAIRES
												HOUDAN
TOTAL CHEVREUSE		36	3	3	0	0	1	5	36	7		
JUVISY 6	1	1	8				6	2	7		CRASH	ETAMPES
		6	1		1						NF BACK UK	WEST MALLING (1 dead)
		5	2						7		FLAK EXPLODED	CORBEIL
		3	3				2		6		CRASH	LIEUSAINT
		6							7		CRASH	BRETIGNY
			6						7		CRASH	MONFORT SUR RISLE
TOTAL JUVISY	1	22	18	1	0	0	7	2	26	7		
MASSY PALAISEAU 8		6							7		CRASH	HOUDAN
		6	1								FRETON	FRETON
		3	1	3					7		CRASH	BONNELLES
		5	1				2	3	2		NF BACK UK	PLAISIR
		5		2			2	2	3		CRASH	LA CELLE
		8					3	4	5		BROKE 2 PARTS	BEAUVAIS
		4	2	1	2				7		CRASH	TACOIGNIERES
									7		CRASH	MONTIGNY LE B
TOTAL MASSY		41	6	7	3	0	7	9	34	7		
VERSAILLES 7		7	1						8		CRASH	LES MESNULS
		2	1	2	3						CRASH TO UK	LISSETT
	1	5		1				7			CRASH	ALLANVILLE (Take off)
		4	2						7		NF	ST CYR
		8	5				4		8		CRASH	BOIS D'ARCY
		5	2					1	2		CRASH	BLEVY
												SOULAIRES
TOTAL VERSAILLES	1	32	11	5	3	0	4	8	32			BOOK
TOTAL NIGHT	1	142	63	16	6	0	25	34	145	24	3 dead in UK	
32		228					204					

Appendix 7 Walter Borchers Victories Claimed.

ANNEXE 8 : LES VICTOIRES DECLAREES PAR WALTER BORCHERS 1940 - 1945

Date	Fname	Lname	Rank	Unit	JG	Claimed	Location	Time	Claim.	Prim_Source	Conf.	Sec_Source
17/05/1940 00:00	Walter	Borchers	Ltn.		4 ZG 76	Morane	.		12,4 1st	1 C.2031/I	Nr.55467/41	OKL
25/05/1940 00:00	Walter	Borchers	Ltn.		4 ZG 76	Spitfire	.		14	2 C.2031/I	Nr.54623/40	OKL
08/06/1940 00:00	Walter	Borchers	Ltn.		4 ZG 76	Hawk-75A	.		17,4	3 C.2031/I	Nr.54623/40	OKL
22/06/1940 00:00	Walter	Borchers	Ltn.		4 ZG 76	Morane	.		17,5	4 C.2031/I	Nr.54627/40	OKL
15/08/1940 00:00	Walter	Borchers	Ltn.		4 ZG 76	Spitfire	S. Salisbury: 3500m		19,05	5 C.2035/II	Amerk: Nr. -	OKL
30/08/1940 00:00	Walter	Borchers	Ltn.		4 ZG 76	Hurricane	.		12,3	6 C.2031/I	Nr.53804/41	OKL
04/09/1940 00:00	Walter	Borchers	Oblt.		4 ZG 76	Spitfire	10km S. London: 3500m		14,05	7 C.2031/I	Nr.54350/41	OKL
04/09/1940 00:00	Walter	Borchers	Oblt.		4 ZG 76	Spitfire	10km S. London: 3500m		14,1	8 C.2095/II	VRE: ASM	OKL
04/09/1940 00:00	Walter	Borchers	Oblt.		4 ZG 76	Spitfire	10km S. London: 3500m		14,35	9 C.2031/I	Nr.54350/41	OKL
11/09/1940 00:00	Walter	Borchers	Oblt.		4 ZG 76	Hurricane	S. Portsmouth: 4500-5000m		17,05	10 C.2035/II	Amerk: Nr.24	OKL
03/03/1943 00:00	Walter	Borchers	Oblt.		8 NJG 3	Wellington	1km W. Launsfært: 3500m [E. Emden]		22,3	7 C.2031/II	Amerk: Nr.52	LW NF Claims
18/03/1943 00:00	Walter	Borchers	Oblt.		8 NJG 3	B-24	50-100km NW JademdundLang: 6500m		15,45	8 C.2031/II	Amerk: Nr 16	LW NF Claims
05/04/1943 00:00	Walter	Borchers	Oblt.	Stab IV.	NJG 1	Wellington	S46 10 in See: 2900m [70km W. Terschelling]		0,46	9 C.2027/	Amerk: Nr 71	LW NF Claims
17/04/1943 00:00	Walter	Borchers	Oblt.	Stab III.	NJG 1	B-17	05 Ost S/74/1 ZG6: 20m		13,52	10 C.2027/I	Amerk: Nr.4	LW NF Claims
24/08/1943 00:00	Walter	Borchers	Hptm.	Stab III.	NJG 5	Stirling	Helenau: 5300m [NE Berlin]		1,14	11 C.2031/II	Amerk: Nr.5	LW NF Claims
01/09/1943 00:00	Walter	Borchers	Hptm.	Stab III.	NJG 5	Stirling	S. Berlin: 4500m		0,5	12 C.2031/II	Amerk: Nr.1	LW NF Claims
04/09/1943 00:00	Walter	Borchers	Hptm.	Stab III.	NJG 5	Lancaster	20km SSE Neuruppin: 4300m		0,45	13 C.2026/I	Amerk: Nr.7	LW NF Claims
09/10/1943 00:00	Walter	Borchers	Hptm.	Stab III.	NJG 5	B-17				14 Caldewell: B. KA		
16/12/1943 00:00	Walter	Borchers	Hptm.	Stab III.	NJG 5	Lancaster	10km NE Berlin: 5800m		20,08	15 C.2031/II	Amerk: Nr 8	LW NF Claims
04/01/1944 00:00	Walter	Borchers	Hptm.	Stab III.	NJG 5	B-24			12,45	15 C.2037 N	445/44. v. 19	LW NF Claims
05/01/1944 00:00	Walter	Borchers	Hptm.	Stab III.	NJG 5	B-24			11,5	17 LW NF Claims 39-45 f. 138		DLC-8:KA
25/05/1944 00:00	Walter	Borchers	Major	7	NJG 5	4-mot. Flzg.	15km W. Aachen: 4800m		0,54	18 C.2027/II	Amerk: Nr. 21	LW NF Claims
08/06/1944 00:00	Walter	Borchers	Major	Stab	NJG 5	4-mot. Flzg.	20km W. Paris: 1300m		2,21	19 C.2037/II	Amerk: Nr.15	LW NF Claims
08/06/1944 00:00	Walter	Borchers	Major	Stab	NJG 5	4-mot. Flzg.	35km W. Paris: 1300m		2,29	20 C.2037/II	Amerk: Nr.16	LW NF Claims
25/06/1944 00:00	Walter	Borchers	Major	Stab	NJG 5	4-mot. Flzg.	30km WSW Paris: 1300m		2,31	21 C.2027/II	Amerk: Nr.17	LW NF Claims
25/06/1944 00:00	Walter	Borchers	Major	Stab	NJG 5	4-mot. Flzg.	QD: 3000m		0,25	22 C.2027/II	Amerk: Nr.19	LW NF Claims
25/06/1944 00:00	Walter	Borchers	Major	Stab	NJG 5	4-mot. Flzg.	N3: 1000m		0,48	23 C.2027/II	Amerk: Nr 20	LW NF Claims
05/07/1944 00:00	Walter	Borchers	Major	Stab	NJG 5	4-mot. Flgz.	05 Ost: N/RE: 2000m [Amiens]		1,5	24 C.2027/II	Amerk: Nr.22	LW NF Claims
16/07/1944 00:00	Walter	Borchers	Major	Stab	NJG 5	4-mot. Flzg.	Châlons-sur-Marne: 1800m		1,35	25 C.2027/II	Amerk: Nr.24	LW NF Claims
29/07/1944 00:00	Walter	Borchers	Major	Stab	NJG 5	4-mot. Flzg.	NW Stuttgart: 4000m		1,58	26 C.2027/II	Amerk: Nr.23	LW NF Claims
14/01/1945 00:00	Walter	Borchers	Oberstltn.	Stab	NJG 5	Lancaster	.			27 LW NF Claims 39-45 f. 230		
14/01/1945 00:00	Walter	Borchers	Oberstltn.	Stab	NJG 5	Lancaster	.			28 LW NF Claims 39-45 f. 230		
14/01/1945 00:00	Walter	Borchers	Oberstltn.	Stab	NJG 5	Lancaster	.			29 LW NF Claims 39-45 f. 230		
15/01/1945 00:00	Walter	Borchers	Oberstltn.	Stab	NJG 5	Lancaster	.			30 LW NF Claims 39-45 f. 230		
15/01/1945 00:00	Walter	Borchers	Oberstltn.	Stab	NJG 5	Lancaster	.			31 LW NF Claims 39-45 f. 230		
15/01/1945 00:00	Walter	Borchers	Oberstltn.	Stab	NJG 5	Lancaster	.			32 LW NF Claims 39-45 f. 230		
06/02/1945 00:00	Walter	Borchers	Oberstltn.	Stab	NJG 5	Lancaster	.			34 LW NF Claims 39-45 f. 234		
08/02/1945 00:00	Walter	Borchers	Oberstltn.	Stab	NJG 5	Lancaster	.			35 LW NF Claims 39-45 f. 234		
06/02/1945 00:00	Walter	Borchers	Oberstltn.	Stab	NJG 5	Lancaster	.			33 LW NF Claims 39-45 f. 234		
05/03/1945 00:00	Walter	Borchers	Oberstltn.	Stab	NJG 5	4-mot. Flzg.	.			37 LW NF Claims 39-45 f. 240		
05/03/1945 00:00	Walter	Borchers	Oberstltn.	Stab	NJG 5	4-mot. Flzg.	.			36 LW NF Claims 39-45 f. 240		

The bombers shot down during the June 7/8 night are highlighted. Walter Borchers claimed 59 victories in total (43 at night).. He was shot down on March 5th 1945 by Walter Gibb near Altenburg (Source: OKL Luftwaffe Claims).

Appendix 8 Je M'Appelais Antoinette – "My name was Antoinette."

A poignant letter written by Anne-Marie Saville de Dudzeele to Mr & Mrs. Baillon, three days after the death of Général de Gaulle en 1970. Gaston Baillon, pork butcher in Gazeran was delivering meat for airmen to Anne-Marie. Our greatest thanks go to "Jo" and Denise Baillon who gave us a copy of the letter (courtesy of Denise Baillon).

TRANSLATION
"My name was Antoinette."

Monsieur, Madame Baillon,

My name was Antoinette then. If I have never forgotten the moments we spent together, it is with the unbearable departure of our General that I come crying with you.
I rang the bell yesterday, in the small isolated chapel above my land, alone, but with the certitude to be heard by all those who have been my true friends.

I kiss you fraternally.

Anne-Marie

Appendix 9 CWGC Commemorative Notices

In Memory of

Flight Sergeant Air Gnr.

John George Shepherd Boanson

1873573, 514 Sqdn., Royal Air Force Volunteer Reserve who died on 08 June 1944 Age 21

Son of Thomas William and Florence Boanson, of Ivinghoe Aston, Buckinghamshire.

Remembered with Honour
La Celle-Les-Bordes Communal Cemetery

Commemorated in perpetuity by
the Commonwealth War Graves Commission

In Memory of

Pilot Officer

Kenneth Edward Bryan

410529, Royal Australian Air Force who died on 08 June 1944 Age 21

Son of Ronald Ernest and Mamie Albertha Bryan, of Geelong East, Victoria, Australia.

Remembered with Honour
La Celle-Les-Bordes Communal Cemetery

Commemorated in perpetuity by
the Commonwealth War Graves Commission

In Memory of

Flight Sergeant Air Gnr.

Robert Calder Guy

1565396, 514 Sqdn., Royal Air Force Volunteer Reserve who died on 08 June 1944 Age 21

Son of Colin Calder Guy and Margaret Park Mathieson Guy, of Glasgow. His brother, Charles Mathieson Guy, also died on service.

Remembered with Honour
La Celle-Les-Bordes Communal Cemetery

Commemorated in perpetuity by
the Commonwealth War Graves Commission

In Memory of

Sergeant

Charles Mathieson Guy

1820355, 514 Sqdn., Royal Air Force Volunteer Reserve who died on 30 July 1944 Age 21

Son of Colin and Margaret Guy, of Glasgow. His brother, Robert Calder Guy also died on service.

Remembered with Honour
Runnymede Memorial

Commemorated in perpetuity by
the Commonwealth War Graves Commission

Appendix 10 Actors

HRH Daisy CLARKE

Mrs Andrée de JONGH

Mrs Anne-Marie ERREMBAULT de DUDZEELE

Mrs Ellen Emily GRANT DALTON, Ken BRYAN billeted family

Angel of CLAIREFONTAINE , Ydoine RIVIERE

Frantzia USANDISAGA, deported to RAVENSBRUCK   † 21/4/1945

AIRMEN Lancaster / Halifax (RAF-RAAF-RCAF) P47-P38 (USAAF)

F/S George BOANSON	MU Gunner	Lancaster MkII DS822	LCLB † 8/6/1944
P/O Ken BRYAN	Wireless Operator	Lancaster MkII DS822	LCLB † 8/6/1944
1st Lt William BUTTNER	Pilot USAAF	P 47 La Villeneuve	LCLB † 15/8/1944
W/O Ken CHAPMAN	Wireless Operator	Lancaster MkIII LM575	
F/S John CLARKE	Flight Engineer	Lancaster MkII DS822	
F/O Jack A N DURHAM	Navigator	Lancaster MkII DS822	
1st Lt Louis GAIGNAT	Pilot USAAF	Pilot USAAF, P 38	CHOISEL † 23/7/1944
F/O Louis GREENBURGH DFC	Pilot	Lancaster MkII LM727	
F/S R C GUY	Rear Gunner	Lancaster MkII DS822	LCLB † 8/6/1944
Sq/L Phil LAMASON RNZAF DFC	Pilot	Lancaster III LM 575	
F/O Bill LEISHMAN RCAF	Navigator	Halifax III LL 863	
P/O Lyndon LEWIS	Bomb Aimer	Lancaster MkII DS822	
F/O William Mc GOWN DFC	Pilot	Lancaster MkII DS822	
1st Lt William Mc GOWAN	Pilot USAAF	P 47	MOON sur ELLE † 6/6/1944
P/O I. V. 'Pop' SEDDON RAAF	Pilot	Halifax III LL 863	
1st LT William SHEPPARD	Pilot USAAF	P 47 La Villeneuve	
F/O Leslie SUTTON DFC	Second Pilot	Lancaster MkII LM727	
F/S John TANNEY	Rear Gunner	Lancaster MkII DS822	

The Boy and the Bomber

RESISTANCE MEMBERS / WARRIORS IN 1944

Paul BIRDSALL (OSS)	London - LCLB	
Gaston BAILLON	Gazeran	
Maurice, Thérèse & Janine CHERBONNIER Comet line	Chevreuse	
Jean DASSIE Comet, BAYONNE deported to BUCHENWALD	Paris	† 25/5/1945
Frédéric de JONGH	Mont Valerien	† 16/2/1945
Doctors A DE PALMA & R DUGUE, Pharmacist M GRISH	Chevreuse	
Priest Fidèle GALLAZZINI	Clairefontaine	
Farmer M GUILLAUMAIN LONGCHENE and all others whose names were not found.		
Juan Manuel LARBURU URRUGNE	Buchenwald	† 16/2/1945
Geneviève PROIX	London WAAF	
Francois PROMPSAUD Comet RAMBOUILLET		
Kenneth WRIGHT RAAF	Mildura	
Ferdinand & Andrée YDIER	LCLB	

WITNESSES

LA CELLE-les-BORDES:	André BILLARD, Johnny BOULE, Monique DACHEUX, Elvire de BRISSAC, Henri KERGREIS, Solange MARCHAL
ST. REMY-lès-CHEVREUSE:	Roger BOSCHET - Suzanne SIFFROI
URRUGNE:	Elisabeth MENDIBURU

Appendix 11 Deer Hunting in LCLB and Landing Points in 1944

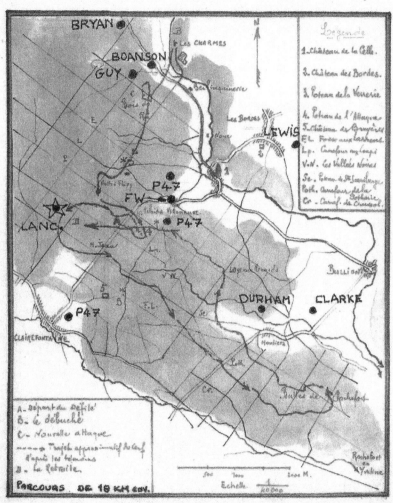

Appendix 12 FAFL Aviators (Forces Aeriennes Francaises Libres) in 1940

22 French Aviators enlisted in RAF in 1940.

14 KIA † "Champ d'Honneur" - 2 Air Accidents
4 Spitfires of FDL group[32] shot down in Somme Bay on September 5th, 1942

Pierre M BLAIZE	1915 - 1941	† English Channel	
Henri BOUQUILLARD	1908 - 1941	† London	
Yves J BRIERE	1919 - 1941	† English Channel	(Only lifejacket recovered)
Maurice CHORON	1911 - 1942	† English Channel	
James DENIS	1906 - 2003		
Victor J DUBOURGEL	1916 - 1942	† * FDL English Channel	Spitfire W 3705
Emile (Francois) FAYOLLE	1916 - 1942	† DIEPPE	
Charles P GUERIN	1916 - 1941	† English Channel	
François de LABOUCHERE	1917 - 1942	† * CAYEUX SUR MER	Spitfire BL 803
Henri G LAFONT	1920 - 2011		
Jean MARIDOR	1920 - 1944	† KENT	
Xavier C. de MONTBRON	1917 - 1955	Killed in DH Vampire crash	1955
René MOUCHOTTE	1914 - 1943	† English Channel	
Georges C PERRIN	1917 - 1981	Shot down 1941 – stopped flying	
Jacques de STADIEU	1914 - 2010		
R A TACONET	1916 - 1942	† * FDL English Channel	Spitfire BM 400
L B THIBAUD	1918 - 1942	† *FDL MERS LES BAINS	Spitfire BL 854
Jacques-Henri SCHLOESING	1919 - 1944	† BEAUVOIR EN LYONS	
Philippe de SCITIVAUX	1911 - 1986		
Georges LE CALVEZ	1918 - 1941	† KOUFRA	
Lionel De MARMIER	1897 - 1944	† MEDITERRANNEE	
Jean DEMOZAY	1915 - 1945	† BUC	

[32] "OKL Claims Luftwaffe" mentions Le Treport or Cayeux sur Mer, low altitude, consistent with RAF archives, "Battle of Britain". FDL (F de Labouchere) was group leader.

Arrived after 1940   (1 KIA, 1 Accident)

Marcel ALBERT	1917 - 2010		Normandie Niemen
Joséphine BAKER	1906 – 1975		Secret Services
Pierre BRISDOUX	1914 - 1944	† UTRECHT	
Pierre CLOSTERMANN	1921 - 2006		1939-1945 Ace
Gustave DOUCHY	1893 - 1943	† MADAGASCAR	1914-1918 Ace
Bernard DUPERIER	1907 - 1995		
Romain GARY	1914 - 1980		
Philippe LIVRY LEVEL	1998 - 1960		
Pierre MENDES France	1907 - 1982		
Roland de la POYPE	1920 - 2012		

Glossary

BBC	British Broadcasting Corporation, London
CIA	Central Intelligence Agency, replaced OSS in 1949
COTAM	Commandement du Transport Aérien Militaire, France
DFC	Distinguished Flying Cross 1 Bar (1550) – 2 Bars (45) – RAF Decoration (numbers awarded in WWII)
DTCA	Direction Technique des Constructions de l'Aéronautique – French Aerospace Technical Direction
FFI	Forces Françaises de l'Intérieur - French Interior Forces
FFL	Forces Françaises Libres (Lorraine Cross) – Free French Forces
FAFL	Forces Aériennes Françaises Libres – Free French Air Forces
FLAK	F lieger A bwerh K anone, German anti-aircraft Defence
Gestapo	**Ge**heime **Sta**ats **Po**lizei - German State Secret Police
MI 5,6,9	Military Intelligence section 5,6,9 English Secret Services
OSS	Office of Strategic Services (US, CIA predecessor in 1940)
RAF	Royal Air Force
RAAF	Royal Australian Air Force
RCAF	Royal Canadian Air Force
RNZAF	Royal New Zealand Air Force

SOE   Special Operations Executive,

USAAF United States Army Air Forces (1941)
           replaced by USAF in 1947

WAAF   Women Auxiliary Air Forces

WRNS   Womens Royal Naval Service.

Lightning Source UK Ltd.
Milton Keynes UK
UKOW05f2009250916

283785UK00007B/176/P